The Art of Raising Children

His Holiness Sri Sri Ravi Shankar

Sri Sri Publications Trust, India

The Art of Raising Children

1st Edition September 2011

ISBN 978 81921798-0-3

Printed in India by Jwalamukhi Mudranalaya Pvt. Ltd., Bangalore
Ph: +91-80-26601064, 26617243

THE ART OF LIVING
Sri Sri Publications Trust
Art of Living International Centre
21st KM, Kanakapura Road, Udaypura, Bangalore – 560082
Phone: +91-80-32722473
Email: info@srisripublications.com
Website: store.artofliving.org

CONTENTS

Chapter 1

THE WHEEL TURNS

One of the most important thing parents should always keep in mind is that at one time they were children too, and that their children will be going through a similar turbulent period that they had gone through, endured and emerged from. They had emerged successfully because of the broad minded understanding that had been shown by their own parents; the love that had enveloped them all times and more so during periods of distress. This understanding and love had never flagged even in the face of periodic rough reactions from them. And that would be one of the main reasons that they themselves have grown up to be good and normal human beings.

Now, the wheel has turned around. And it is the turn of the once-upon-a-time children who have grown up to become parents themselves to show the same, if not greater, understanding and love. They need to build up that trust in their children which will ensure that they will be consulted regarding everything – from advice on subjects and careers to be chosen to spats with boyfriends or girlfriends!

Teachers are, ideally, extensions of parents in school. Most teacher-student relations do not take off due to disinterest on the part of the teacher and/or fear and apprehension on the part of the student. This 'extension of hand' for a warm 'shake' has to first come from the teacher for the simple reason that they are older and need to set an example.

Children are ever watching the teachers and will emulate most of what they say or do. And when something wrong is emulated and is pointed out by parents at home, children tend to dispute its wrongness by pointing out that their teacher too had said or done so.

The world has shrunk and now it is multi-cultural and multi-faith. A student, after his education, may need to take up a job in any corner of the world. He would need to be comfortable doing so. For this he needs to be open and broad minded. Education alone can bring out these qualities. They will not suddenly sprout forth in the last few years of college. The seeds need to be sown from the very first day in school and nurtured well thenceforth. Only then the children will grow up to be strong 'trees' of broad-mindedness; who will not be shaken by the strongest of storms; who will accept everybody in the world as their very own. This has to be jointly accomplished by the parents and the teachers.

Chapter 2

ADDING VALUE TO EDUCATION

oday, it is the concern of every parent that their children grow up to be well-educated human beings with certain values in their lives. These days if you ask children how many friends they have, they will count on their fingers - one, two, three, four, five... Not more than that. If you don't know how to be friendly with the 40-50 children present in your classroom, how will you ever become friendly with the six billion people on this planet? The basic tendency to be friendly is lost somewhere in the pursuit of selfish education.

It's high time that we came together to identify ways and means of restoring the respect, honour and dignity that education has commanded historically. The need of the day is a broad-minded education accompanied by a warm heart. It is of no use if you acquire good education and then look down upon everybody else. A well-educated person is the one who is friendly and compassionate, who can be a 'nobody' with everybody. Obsolete principles, theories, systems of education and methodologies of transmitting knowledge need to undergo a change. Today you need not memorise the multiplication tables. If the same outdated method of education is followed in our schools and colleges, it is a waste of time. In this computer age, one can know all about history with just a click. Still children spend hours and hours learning when the Mutiny happened and carry books, on their backs - huge loads of books on irrelevant subjects. By the time a child enters college, he or she is already worn out.

We need to harness a child's capacity to digest more, understand more instead of just bombarding them with a lot of unwanted information. Sadly, we have not done anything to increase the capacity of our consciousness. Creative methods of teaching will help children build their personalities. Creative sports and ancient techniques such as meditation, *yoga* and *pranayama* should be a part of a child's learning process. The education system should prevent people from becoming fanatics. The right education must harness a mind that is free, not obsessed with anything and neither angry about the past nor worried about the future. A good system of education must instill self-esteem and creativity. We have to instill confidence in education, broaden the vision and deepen the roots. Everybody who has a stake in education must ponder on a holistic, healthy education system that will retain the virtues and values which we all are naturally endowed with. Education must attend to all facets of human life. The key is to harness the ancient and be innovative with the modern. Only an education that can nourish in built virtues can impart true intelligence.

Chapter 3

ROLE OF THE PARENTS

I. Multifarious Activities

*C*hildren need to be exposed to multifarious activities. This has to be done early in life. They need to be exposed to science, arts, etc and activities that develop all the faculties, like doing service. On any Sunday, they can be given some chocolates and asked to distribute them to the poor children. Once or twice in a year, they can be taken to a slum to do social service. This will enhance their personality.

The concept of *Saraswati*, the Goddess of Learning, is very amazing. If you look at the figure of the Goddess, you will see that She is holding a musical instrument, a book and a rosary. The book symbolizes nourishing the left brain which deals with science, the musical instrument symbolizes nourishing the right brain which deals with arts and the rosary symbolizes the meditative aspect. Knowledge, music and meditation – all three are required to make an education complete. Only then can a person be educated and civilized. So, it is essential that children learn music and *yoga*.

II. Scientific Temperament

They should be encouraged to have a scientific temperament and also to ask questions. A child starts asking questions from the age of three. Often, they come up with questions for which parents may not have any answers. This will make them wonder and ponder on the reality which they find stunning. So, it is very necessary for them to adopt a scientific temperament.

III. Interaction

They should be encouraged to interact with various age groups: younger than them, the same age as them and older to them as well. This is very important and will indicate whether they are developing any superiority or inferiority complex or if they are becoming introverted or extroverted. They can be moulded to be very balanced, talented and flexible human beings; having personalities free of complexes. Children with inferiority complexes like to interact more with those younger to themselves. They will try to avoid the older ones and may even try to avoid those of the same age. And those with superiority complex will try to shun the younger ones and will only want to relate to ones older to them. In either case they will not be good communicators. The parents can teach them communication skills. It is very important for them to learn how to communicate well.

IV. Children and Yoga

All children should have a dream if they wish to reach the heights that they aspire to. Only then will they achieve their goals in life. Their growth should be intuned with the service of the society and the country; to make it strong and bring about a change in the world for the betterment of all. They should practice *pranayama* because it helps one to concentrate more. Applying *chandan* on the forehead will help them activate the pituitary gland. This will bring out calmness and will improve memory. They should learn around ten *shlokas* and recite them daily. Doing *yoga* will help them to be happy, healthy, skilful and smart. They should adopt the practice of meditating, singing some light *bhajans* early in the morning and before sleeping. These are simple ways to have a stress-free life.

If a child is not mischievous when young then how can that be a childhood! They should have the confidence to speak without nervousness. Children who regularly fight amongst themselves should join the military. If they have to fight, they should fight for the country! Instead of fighting with each other they should be friendly with all. They need to share with all.

V. Fun and Boredom

How children feel when the week begins on Monday and how they feel when it ends on Friday shows how much they have grown; how much they are relating themselves at school. Some of them wait eagerly for the weekend and some for Monday to get back to school. When school is not fun, they will wait for the weekend to have some fun. They may feel that there is no freedom in school and that is the reason it is not fun. When something is forced on their minds, there will be boredom. A little later they will stop liking what they had intended to do. A change can get rid of the boredom. They will like to read books on the subjects that they are not studying. Reading such topics will be interesting and informative.

VI. Friendliness with Teachers

A teacher is not just the one who preaches, but the one who takes the students along. The difference between a preacher and teacher is that a preacher just preaches and need not necessarily practice his preaching while a teacher lives his teachings. Students can consult their teachers about anything that they feel they can't handle by themselves. Teachers wait for the students to come forward and shake hands first. They have their own limitation - if they forward their hands and the students don't, then they will feel embarrassed. To avoid this they wait for the students to take the first step.

A student should try to see things from the teacher's point of view. He can imagine that he is a teacher and he has twenty students in his class. How would he handle them? Then he will find that the teachers are not cold but are very warm. Even if they are not warm, he can warm them up if he has enough warmth in himself! A student just needs to talk to his teachers and feel the closeness; feel a sense of belongingness. It brings a big change in the atmosphere. When we were in school we were so attached to our teachers even from the first grade. We would give a gift to them every day - a flower or something else. We felt very close to them. We used to wait eagerly to see them after vacations. Often, while on vacation, we would go to our teachers' homes just to chat for a while.

Teachers help develop the students' personalities and make them blossom fully. The students can drop all the inhibitions; all the walls that get built up consciously or unconsciously.

VII. Friendliness among Themselves

Making a new friend every day can make school life great fun. There may be twenty or thirty students in a class. Would they be on friendly terms and close to everybody in the class? Most probably not. If they cannot be friendly with everybody in their class then how can they be friendly with the whole world when they leave the school? Their ability to make friends is very limited. A school is a place where they can enhance this ability - meet so many students and be friends with them. If they can take a decision that they will make a new friend every day, or every week, then something in them will blossom. This is real education. Real education will strongly develop their personalities and will ensure that they relate well with people around them.

What is it that stops students from being friendly with everyone? It is the feeling of what other people think about them. If they have any such apprehensions, then they should go out and shake hands with them. They should talk to them and see how they can get over the barriers. These barriers are their own creation and should be got over in the very beginning. As children grow older, it becomes harder. They can develop the ability of being friendly. It is a wonderful thing. They need to get over their embarrassment. They should not think what the other person will think of their overtures; whether they will acknowledge them and respond to their friendliness; whether they will get hurt and lose their self-esteem. The students need to put aside all such thoughts and doubts and greet someone whom they do not know and thus make a new friend. This can make their personalities blossom. They could keep a diary and record in it how many friends they make in a year. Several billion people live on this planet, and in our whole lifetime we meet or come cross a few hundred or may be a few thousand. And of all these people that we meet, we talk to very few, and among those few that we talk to, we make friends with very few.

VIII. Belongingness

In the school there are several games which are played. One of the games is changing the names of the players. A student exchanges his name with a friend for three weeks. They have a lot of fun. Students should feel one with everyone in their schools; feel so with lots of love and oneness. They have the capacity to do this. They should feel close to all the teachers in the school - feel that they belong to the teachers and the teachers belong to them; feel a personal connection with the school and consider it not just a public property. Students should feel at home in all groups; in all age groups of people; with all cultures. That will make them grow and blossom. The mind, intellect and heart will grow into a complete personality. If these points are considered, it will be realized how lives can be enriched by living them.

IX. Internal Support in the Group

Students should support the weakest in their group. If everyone helps those who are weak in anything, in games or in studies, then they will not feel the weakness. Suppose in the soccer team one member is very weak and all others who are very proficient support him, then he will forget his weakness. He will feel the strength even though he is not strong. Then he too will start supporting someone who has failed. And if others have the same attitude, he will get all the support whenever he needs it. Nobody wants pity and compassion. All they want is friendliness. Even if some support is given it should be given in such a way that it is not felt by the recipient.

There is a story about a wise man from Persia. Once he was drowning in a river and was saved by one of his friends. And after that day, this friend would always remind that wise man - how he had saved his life. He would tell him not to ever forget it. Finally, the wise man got frustrated. He took his friend back to the same spot. He told him that he was going sink in the water and was going to save himself! So, the friend should not tell him again that he had saved his life! Students should not try to cash in on the support of friends. It is the main reason why they don't come forward to support. They should just be very friendly with them. If someone is shy, one should go along with them. It will be a very good way to open up with people.

X. Non-Reactive Temperament

Everyone is like a machine. If someone presses a button, they flare up. Another person pushes another button and they react in another way. They become predictable machines. Students should be unpredictable. Then they will have a lot of fun in life. There is a lot of fun to have every day, whether in school or outside. When they feel right in their minds – fresh, light and happy, then they will do very well in their studies. They will be able to comprehend something after studying it just once.

XI. Laughter

Another point is to laugh, come what may. A student may think that he or she may fail in an examination. Then, it should be decided that the first thing that will be done when the failure is known is to laugh. Whether the student passes or fails, it should be decided to laugh. Then there will be de-conditioning. I made a program for children in India. I made them take seven oaths. The first oath was to laugh. For one month, I made them all take these oaths. They might come crashing down the stairs, but the first thing that they would do was - laugh. Everything could fall apart, but the first thing would be laughter. They enjoyed this very much. The idea is to laugh at whatever happens. Then, something very profound in life will be achieved. There is nothing great in laughing when everything is going well. Everybody does it anyway. But someone who is educated, who is strong and whose personality is flowering should be able to laugh when everything falls apart. This is because laughter gives the strength to manage any situation. This should be done for one month. Even if someone hurls an insult the first response should be - laugh.

Students can solve any problem when they take it as a challenge. What is the difference between a problem and a challenge? If something is considered a problem, then the concerned person is a part of the problem and not a part of the solution. But if something is considered a challenge, then the person is a part of the solution rather than the problem. A challenge is an adventure. What is an adventure? Is an adventure not a problem? Students go on adventure trips. They do mountaineering or other such thing. It is as a student, one can go on many adventures and be adventurous.

Students have to be very naughty. Being naughty is good. They may have been told often not to be so. But, they should be naughty. They should have fun. Then, their personalities will bloom. However, this fun should not be at the cost of someone else.

XII. Science and Arts

Students need to study a bit of both: the science and the arts. If one tends to be more oriented towards the arts, then some effort should be made to develop some interest in the science. A visit to a science museum could trigger such an interest. Then, again if there is a great inclination towards science then one could be encouraged to take an interest in the arts, music, painting, sculpture, etc. It is not very difficult to get students interested in music because they do have an artistic side to them. However, boys will need a little more encouragement in this than girls. The latter have a natural inclination towards arts.

Students can be engaged in suitable projects where they will contribute; where they will be giving rather than acquiring or possessing.

XIII. Precautions

If students are not able to concentrate on their studies, they need to watch out for the following:
1. Diet - They should have a balanced diet. It makes a big difference.
2. Physical exercises – This is essential. If physical exercises are not done then the blood circulation will be affected. There will be a tendency to be lazy and they will not feel like studying. So, it is

necessary to do a little bit of physical exercise, some *yoga*, *pranayama* and meditation. They can also participate a little in singing. The needs of the body will be furnished, and then the learning and retaining capacity will increase. They will be able to study as well as gain much more in a shorter period of time.

Chapter 4

PARENTING, A TWO WAY JOURNEY

Parenting, A Two Way Journey
7 June 2010
Bangalore Ashram, India

*I*t is very difficult for me to talk about parenting. I have no experience. But I can give you some ideas from my observation. You have to put this into your experience and see.

1.   If you are very orderly, children will make you chaotic. Children are the best to break your boundaries. I remember one of my uncles was strict and used to discipline me and my sister all the time. When he had a son, his son started disciplining him, broke all his barriers. So, your children teach you a lot that others may not be able to. The first thing for us is to observe the kid, its tendencies, and the direction the child is taking. It is a two way journey. What do you want to learn from them? And what do you want to teach them? Don't force your vision on them. Share your vision with them and persuade them if their vision is wrong. Every child comes to this planet with certain tendencies, certain basics which cannot be changed. And he/she acquires certain things which can be controlled.

It is a big exercise. If you are a very disciplined person, children can create chaos in your life, break your barriers.

2.   We have to be very sensitive. This is one thing that we have to keep in our mind. If you tell children not to lie, and ask them to reply a phone call saying you are not at home, this is simply not going to work. Having an argument in front of your children will make it worse. If you want to have some argument between you and your spouse, you better give some job to your children sned them away, and then fight as much as you want. But by the time they come back, you better patch up.

3.   We encourage the tendency in children to not to share things and hold on to them. When that goes beyond a certain limit, we feel suffocated. Then they develop this tendency of holding back. It can be a hindrance. Small actions can reflect one's personality. At the same time we can encourage their giving and sharing attitude and that can develop their personality. So, we can do a lot in modifying the acquired personality traits of a child. But you cannot do anything with the seed that a child is born with. That will come anyway. These two aspects we have to distinguish, and that is wisdom. And half the job is done if you can do that. The other half, you have to leave to God. You have no control on the other half. So this whole process teaches a lot of patience and perseverance, and yet leading them to where they should be going.

4.   Giving them a dream and persuading them to walk towards the dream is one of the biggest challenges in front of the parents.

5.   I want you to do an exercise. Tell the person sitting next to you, "I don't trust you". This is a good opportunity to say it if the person is your spouse (laughter)! (After some time when audience couldn't do it even after being asked two – three times) You cannot

do it seriously. See how difficult it is to tell someone that you don't trust them. It is difficult to tell someone that you trust them. But it is even more difficult to tell someone that you don't trust them. Did you get it? Did you notice you did something that you have never done before? You told someone that you don't trust them and you started smiling. Has this ever happened to you before? Children have a tendency to trust by nature. But somehow their trust is broken. We need to look into that. Do they trust themselves? Do they have enough confidence in themselves?

A healthy child will have three kinds of trust - trust in divinity, trust in the goodness of people and trust in oneself. A healthy child will not think that everybody is a thief or everybody is bad. He/She does not get into this sort of paranoia. A healthy child knows that people are good. A healthy child has trust in himself/ herself and trust in the unseen power of God, Divinity or some higher power. These three types of trust can make a child genius. These are the ingredients to make a very talented and genius child. To nurture them, we need to bring about these tendencies in them.

If you keep telling children that everyone is a cheat, the child loses trust in the people around and society in general. Their personality, talents and communication skills will shrink. Their interaction with people will suffer a great deal. They become unsuccessful business persons, unsuccessful professionals and unsuccessful artists. They may have talents but this is the result you will get if trust in people and in the goodness of things as they are is taken away. Today, you have many young people who want to be entrepreneurs but they are not successful. You know why? This is the reason. They neither trust the goodness of people nor do they trust themselves. As parents we have to develop these things in a child. Do you encourage if they come to you with complaints? What do you do? Do you encourage the negativity? Or you mould it to something positive. You have to play a balanced role. Sometimes your child comes to you and says so and so is so good and that friend is not so good. Here you have to point out their mistakes and bring them to the center. If they get swayed away by somebody and you know whose habits are not so good, then you have to tell the negative things. But if they are telling you negative things about somebody, then you have to point out the positive. So, you have to do a balancing act; whenever a child swings too much to the left or too much to the right. Do you agree with me? We create an atmosphere around us. If we create an atmosphere of trust and children grow in that atmosphere, they become brilliant. But, if we create an atmosphere of negativity, distrust, or dejection, they are going to reflect and bounce the same thing on us. Having come here today, I want to give you an exercise to do which I want you to do every day. When you come back from work and meet your children, the first thing you do is clap with them or play or laugh. It may look a little artificial for a day or two. But later on, it will become a breakthrough for you and your kids. Sit and have food with the whole family as often as possible or at least 3 to 4 times a week. And while having food, don't tell them they are bad. While serving them food, don't put off their moods. There is a time to tell them that they are wrong, but never on the dining table.

Close your eyes for 30 seconds. Just suppose that everyone is telling you that they don't trust you. Think no one trusts you. How do you feel?(After 30 seconds) Open your eyes. Bad, sad, unhappy! You know this is the atmosphere we create - 'I don't trust you, I don't trust you'. It is an effort to create a healthy atmosphere. I understand your life is not just your children. You have so many other things; you have to interact with so many other people. When you have no control over your own moods, it is difficult to make a mood or create an atmosphere just for the sake of children. But we need to make an effort.

So, let us quickly go over it once again.

a) Have dinner with the children at least 3-4 times in a week. And when you are having food, don't point out their mistakes or blame them. See that their mood is uplifted.

b) See that their personality is so developed that they don't feel the generation gap. They must interact with the elders as well as the youngsters. Give them some responsibility of the youngsters and sometimes something to do for the older ones, like this you can bridge the generation gap.

c) Engage them in some project where they are contributing, they should be giving rather than acquiring or possessing. We need to do something to inculcate this tendency in children. Just small things, it need not be anything big.

d) See that they have three types of trust: trust in themselves, trust in society; and trust in the divinity. Sometimes they say, "I can't do it." Encourage them and tell them that they can do it. Trust in the goodness of people. Tell them the stories or good happenings in the world, not just the negative things. If they grow up with the feeling of mistrust or fear, there will be paranoia. Their personality will start shrinking, they will never blossom, they will never be good communicators in the society. Trust the society and trust in divinity. A little bit of ritual is essential to create an atmosphere for children. Make them sit and do some chanting. Ask them to light a candle or a lamp, some little bit of ritual is good for them to hold on to. Make them break a coconut or go to the temple. It is important to root a little bit of *sanskara*, about something that is supernatural. A faith in the unknown can take them a long way. Not too much though, just a little bit. Make them read a few *shlokas*. These things will develop their personality.

e) When children are very positive about their friends, give them a little caution, but not too much. If they are very negative about some friends, show that there is something positive out there too. In this way, you are pushing them to the center, not letting them fall on either side.

f)Learn from them. Don't always stand up as a teacher but participate and learn from them.

Chapter 5

AVOIDING PARENTING TRAPS

*T*here are certain steps that can be taken to bring out the best in children.

I. Parents should cultivate the habit of sharing in children. It is latent in them but is not encouraged. Instead, when they are given toys, gifts or chocolates they are usually told to keep those to themselves and not to give them away. This is not good as it shrinks the child's personality. They should be told to share with everybody.

II. The second point is to let them have more friends. Let them be free and drop their inhibitions. Let them meet and talk to everybody.

III. The third point is to teach them to tolerate criticism. It will make them strong. It is alright if they cry sometimes. Often parents think that the children should not cry, therefore they pamper them. This is not good. Crying is a kind of breathing that helps to open up the lungs. If children are not allowed to cry, they will not know how to release the pent-up emotions. A child who does not cry gets depressed. A child who laughs and cries freely cannot get depressed. There is a difference between a depressed child and a sad one. A child may cry for some time and then will be happy again. But a child who does not cry or is not allowed to cry will become moody. When children want to cry, they will find an excuse to do so. They may ask for something and when that is given to them, they will ask for something else. They may appear to be making a fuss but it is not so. They just want an excuse to cry. Parents may try to pacify them by giving them many things because they like to see their children smiling. But this will not work. Children in this situation should be told that they will not be given anything and they may cry if they wish.

Sometimes a child cries a lot. Then the parents also should start crying with them; louder than them! Then, child will stop. This is another trick you should know. Parents tend to forget that children like crying at times and that it is good for their health.

IV. They can be told good stories and nonviolence can be nurtured in them. It can be pointed out to them that even animals have life. Children believe that animals have all the emotions. That sensitivity should be maintained. When we were children I would see some boys catching hold of the colourful butterflies and putting them in small matchboxes. They would also tie them with a thread. I would tell them that they should not do this as butterflies have life, too. When they were distracted by something else I would set the butterflies free.

Children tend to throw stones at dogs. But I could never do it nor could I tolerate other children doing it. People just throw stones at stray dogs or torture them. All animals have life and we can make children sensitive to life. Then, they will have more compassion.

Parents should turn a deaf ear to their children's pleas for toys like guns. Neither should they allow their children to see violent movies and serials. Violence needs to be checked for children. This is because when they see it often, it becomes something ordinary for them. Then, a shooting or a stray bullet killing somebody seems something ordinary. Of course, it cannot be avoided totally.

V. There is no need to give children pocket-money. In our younger days, we had a bowl in our home in which some money was kept. If we needed anything, we would take some money from it and put the change back into it after our purchase. And we would tell our parents how much money we had taken. We were never given any fixed pocket money. Money was always available in the bowl. So, there was never an idea of 'my' money. Children who get a regular pocket money get so attached to it for no reason. When they grow up they tend not to care for their parents or elders. Then, nothing else is as important for them as money. This is a habit we nurture in them. We can change it.

VI. They should be made to feel that they will get whatever they need. There needs to be a sense of abundance in them from the beginning. They should have trust and faith and pray every morning and night. They can be told that they can pray for whatever they want. If a girl wants a doll then she can pray for it and God will give her one. A habit of prayer can be cultivated in them rather than making demands. Some children will throw tantrums for anything that they want. They can be asked to pray to God for whatever they want - a doll, a toy, etc. When they pray they will cultivate the habit of asking rather than throwing tantrums. Of course, you cannot totally avoid these tantrums but you can reduce the frequency and prevent the child from becoming an emotional wreck. Otherwise, they will be excessively aggressive all the time.

VII. Some aggression in a child is normal. You don't want your child to turn totally into a vegetable. Let the child rebel. It is good if they rebel sometimes. And you should not be a goody-goody parent all the time. A mother should also fight with the child sometimes. It is good and healthy. Otherwise if a child has never fought with anybody at home and then comes face to face with somebody outside wanting to fight, it will be a totally new phenomenon and he/she may end being a loser. Nothing should be done in excess! If there is fighting all the time then their nature will become very unfriendly. If you do fight then you should make up quickly and cheer them up. They should forget their fighting mood and come back to the present moment. You should do that, too. You may show anger but should not hold on to it. That is a healthy life. If you want to be 'goody-goody' all the time and never willing to punish your child then it is not going to work. When they grow up, the children themselves will tell you that you have been a hopeless mother. They will ask you why you did not set them right at the appropriate time.

Children imitate their mothers. If the mother is serious they look serious too. If the mother is happy and smiling, the children are so, too. So, you need to have a balanced attitude. I have seen people speak with such sugary sweetness to their children in some of the very wealthy families in India. All kinds of endearments are used and the child feels so sick hearing them! It just wants to get out of there! Being extra polite and over-sweet all the time is not going to work. It will create a gulf between the parents and the child.

There is an old proverb in India – 'Once your daughter or son becomes sixteen, treat them like a friend. Don't be a parent anymore.' So, your parenthood is limited till the children are fifteen or sixteen. After that you need to forget that you are a parent and treat them like a friend. That is the correct attitude with children. Till then if you need to put your foot down, you can do so.

VIII. Some strictness will bring about discipline in them and they will be happy.

One of my uncles was very strict with us. He would confiscate all the chocolate boxes that were given to us. He would then give us just one chocolate a day after we had completed all our homework. We had to read an English newspaper. English was not so commonly used in those days either in the households or in the schools. The local languages were used most often. Our uncle would force us to read English. It was such a pain! The pronunciations were so difficult for us. We would argue with him about certain pronunciations, eg. the word 'know'. We would argue that the 'k' needed to be pronounced, too. I would rebel and would not get a chocolate. His weekly holiday used to be on Thursday and he would be at home in the afternoon. That day, we would have no freedom. We had to study all the words. Sometimes I would write them in our own script - *Kannada* which is phonographic, ie, a word is pronounced as it is written. Of course, at that time we resented our uncle for being so strict. But it was a blessing in disguise! We did not have too many chocolates and had good teeth! And we became fluent in English.

If you look back, you will realize that you scored well in the classes of those teachers who were very strict and not so well in the classes of those who were very slack and did not insist on your studying. Of course when our strict uncle had a son, he was not strict with him. If he cried, he was immediately given many chocolates. And he did not have good teeth! He got into all sorts of bad eating habits. Discipline in that sense is very good. In the beginning you may resist but you will get used to it. But, everything should have a limit. It is like riding a horse. You have to keep holding the rein. If you leave it totally, the horse will not be under your control. If you hold it too tight, then it will not move. So, as required, sometimes you may have to hold the reins tight and sometimes you may have to let it loose. We need to take the same attitude with children. Do not feel bad if you get angry with your child on a particular day. Just make sure you show more love the next day.

IX. Food plays a big role in a child's development. Parents often fall prey to the demands of their children and give them heavy food that is hard to digest. This adversely affects their attention and retention. It would be good if parents give the children light breakfasts before sending them to school. This will ensure that they will not feel sleepy.

Chapter 6

BRINGING INNOCENCE BACK INTO OUR LIVES

"Bringing innocence back into our lives"
Peter Maffay Conference, Germany
May 2010

We are all children in some sense. I wish we are more of a child than an adult. You know, a child smiles 400 times a day, adolescent smiles 17 times and an adult does not smile at all. There will be very less conflicts in the world if only people in the world can smile more.

We have been discussing the problem of violence and conflicts in the world since morning. What is the solution? Where are we heading to? We grew up with the ideology of Mahatma Gandhi. We used to attach pride in being non-violent. Unfortunately, today, the pride is associated with aggression and violence. Someone who is aggressive and loses temper easily is considered heroic in schools and colleges. We need to make the shift from attaching pride to violence to attaching pride to non-violence. We need to give our children a global vision of a violence-free and stress-free society. I am sure we can achieve this by incorporating these five things:

1. First thing is music and dance.

2. Second is sports. With the advent of computer and video games, children don't go out and play as they used to do before. They lock themselves up with the video games, most of which are violent. We need to give an orientation to make sports more popular.

3. Third is travel. We conduct programs in India, America, sometimes in Europe, Poland, Germany, also here in Black Forest, where we bring children from all the countries together for a week. Many a times, they speak their own language, but just being with each other creates such a bonding between them that the barriers melt down and they feel at home. We should help them travel around and communicate with people of other cultures and religions. We need to give children multi-cultural and multi-religious education. I feel all the children should know a little bit about all the knowledge in the world – Hinduism, Buddhism, Judaism, Christianity, Catholicism, Shaoism, Shintoism. A little understanding of all the major religions and cultures of the world helps them grow up with a broader mindset. Even if a small part in the world is left with people thinking that only they are right, the world will not be a safe place to live. The sense of belongingness, that we belong to one global family in spite of different colours, languages and food habits, has to be developed in children and youth.

4. Fourth thing is involving children in some service projects. There is such an opening that happens in youth when they are associated with some service project.

5. Then is *yoga* and meditation. I have made *yoga* so secular that people from any religious background will have no objection in doing it. It is just some breathing techniques and some postures, not attached to any belief system.

Our breath is linked to our emotions. For every emotion, there is a particular rhythm in the breath. So, when you cannot directly harness your emotions, with the help of breath you can do it. If you are in a theater, you would know that a director asks you to breathe faster when you have to show anger. If you have to show a serene scene, the director would tell you to breathe softer and slower. If we understand the rhythm of our breath, we are able to have a say over our mind, we can win over any negative emotions like anger, jealousy, greed, and we are able to smile more from our heart. I think we need to bring the childlike beauty and innocence, that God gifted every human being, back into our lives.

Now, I want to narrate an incident. Two years ago, we had a group of 200 youths from Arab countries that came to Bangalore. At the same time, we had about 35 youths from Israel also. When the Arab youth came to know that there were youth from Israel also, they turned so violent, wild and angry that they were ready to pack their luggage and leave. But it took us less than a couple of hours to sit and talk to them, during which they learnt some breathing exercises, meditation and a little bit of *yoga* and they became such good friends at the end of the third day. At the end of the week, the two groups had tears in their eyes while departing from each other. Their experiences are worth listening to.

Chapter 7

HUMAN VALUES IN THE CLASSROOM

The teaching profession is one of the best. It is also a very big responsibility. As a teacher you have to set an example because children watch you carefully. Only half of the values they learn from their parents and the rest are from their teachers. Children observe much more than adults. They observe everything you say and do. They observe when you are calm and composed, and when you are tensed and unsmiling. They watch and imitate you. Their behaviour patterns depend to a great extent on those of the parents and to the some extent on those of their teachers.

Parents may have to deal with only one or two children but teachers have many more in their classrooms. The situation is more testing and stressful. To handle it, you need to centre yourself a few times every day. Just before lunch you should sit and calm yourself. You should have a deep trust that everything is being taken care of or will be taken care of; that you have been assigned a job which you can handle.

First of all, you need to trust yourself. If you think you have a very big task that you cannot handle, then you will really not be able to handle it. You need to think that the task you have is appropriate for you and that you will handle it to the best of your ability. A lot of patience is necessary. It would be good to sit and relax and just be with nature for a short time every day. You can start meditating regularly to increase your energy. A few deep breaths will also help.

Basic human values need to be encouraged in the classroom. A child is born with these values and teachers need to uncover them. The human values are compassion, co-operation, friendliness, smile, laughter, lightness, helping nature, belongingness, caring for each other, etc. These need to be nourished and brought out. Often, teachers need to de-program some of the behaviour children would have learnt at home. Any negativity you find in a child is really only on the periphery. It is not its real nature. With loving attention and care you can bring out the positive human values in it.

This is true even for rebellious children. They need more physical contact, more encouragement and more pats on the back. They need to be made to feel that they are loved, that you really care for them and that they belong. On the other hand, with children who are very timid and shy you can use a little firmness to help them stand up and speak out. You can be a little tough with them and, at the same time, you can be loving. It is rather a delicate process - firmness coupled with love.

Often the reverse is done. Teachers are strict with rebellious children and liberal with shy ones. Then, because they are used to being treated that way, the shy ones remain that way all their lives. Involving children in active games is helpful. Restless children need a lot of exercises.

In Ayurvedic medicine, three personality types are dealt with. The first type is *vata*. *Vata* children tend to be thin and very restless. They will be quick to learn and also quick to forget. They need a lot of exercise to reduce the *vata* tendencies. The second type is *pitta*.

Pitta children have a medium build, are steady and sharp in their studies. They remember well but have a short temper. The third type is *kapha*. *Kapha* children tend to be physically bulky. They will be slow in learning but will not forget what they learn. You can usually look at the body structure and identify their appropriate type. Each type needs different handling.

Educating a child should be holistic and not just a process of stuffing their heads with information. Just coming to class and learning a few lessons is not really the education that a child needs. We have to see to the total development of the body and the mind because they are linked. The body and mind are so linked that what we put in the body reflects in the mind and what is in the mind reflects in the body and in its actions. Human values need to be cultured for the sake of the mind and the body. These principles are the basis on which you can start building your idea of human values.

In the Canadian Schools, the child who is the friendliest in the classroom gets an award. I think this is the first country that has instituted such an award. It is a good system and can be emulated by schools all over the world. It encourages children to be friendly with everybody. Usually, children sit in the same place in the class every day. This is not a good idea because they get very attached to that place. When some other kid comes and sits there they quarrel. They think of their seat as their personal place. They don't feel that they 'own' every seat in the classroom. They just 'own' their own chair and become very possessive about it. They can be told to sit in different places and next to different children every day. It is the teachers who are responsible for making them sit in the same place every day. It is for their convenience. But this bereft children from having a sense of belongingness with everybody in the class. It does make things a little more difficult for the teachers. But it is better for the children's growth.

The child who ranks the highest may be made to sit with the child having the lowest rank and asked to help. Usually all the children having higher ranking sit in one group and the lower ranking ones in another group. This is also not healthy for the classroom atmosphere. Once the higher ranking children start relating to the lower ranking ones, they begin to develop a feeling of belongingness with each other. And there is a greater sense of love and caring among them.

A sense of sharing can be developed in them. There are many ways to do this. Around the world, we conduct a program called ART Excel (All Round Training for Excellence) that includes all these principles. In the five day ART Excel course (often taught at summer camps) children are given some processes and exercises to reinforce their values and strengthen their sense of self. We inculcate nonviolence in them. This program brings a big change in them. A child who has done three or four ART Excel courses learns to smile in every situation. Even if someone insults them, they will smile. Of course, sometimes parents have problem with this. After doing the ART Excel course, children just smile when their parents get annoyed with them. Then, they feel that the children don't mind their scolding. But then the parents are also unable to stay grim and they start smiling, too. When a child is insulted, it usually feels like crying. But we teach the participants of ART Excel to just smile at whoever insults them. When they do that, they are on the way to overcome reacting.

Another technique we encourage is to greet the person who insults. Then, the person who insults feels a shift taking place. He or she is surprised that the one they have insulted has greeted them instead of reacting and getting angry. This brings about a sense of nonviolence and a big change in them. The sense of nonviolence is generated in them and the root of violence starts eliminating. When I was in school, anyone who even spoke about guns was looked down upon.

Every student deplored it. And if anyone shouted or lost his or her temper, they would be looked down upon, too. Such outbursts were so abnormal that the concerned person would feel ashamed of it. Nowadays, there is no such thing and those values have vanished.

The same applied to the teachers, too. A teacher even giving a student a stern look was something very uncommon because there was so much love between them. There was a tradition that once a week a student had to give a gift the teacher - a flower, a fruit, a homemade sweet, etc. Every class would have a table that was covered with flowers. These values and practices are not there anymore. To bring them back, we may have to educate children in programs outside school. Having teachers enforce these traditions as new rules will not work. Some other person will have to educate them on how to respect their teachers more. This can be done in summer camps. When someone other than parents and teachers are taking care of the children then new ideas and new values can be taught. We have to teach children the value of the sense of belongingness with one's parents and teachers. Students need to take pride in their teachers. A sense of belongingness with the teacher and a teacher-student relationship should be established. If this is not important then they can just learn their lessons from a computer. There is no need for a human presence in the form of a teacher. The presence of a teacher gives a human touch. That is what we need to sustain and develop in the classroom. We need to strengthen this human touch; this human connection.

When compiling class timetables, teachers should do so in a way that can bring out the best in the children. It is better not to have a subject like history immediately after lunch in the afternoon session. After lunch, it would be good to have a class where the children do not need to just listen. Their attention and listening capacity goes down after a meal. They would rather sleep than sit and listen. If you have a crafts class immediately after lunch then they will be active physically and will not feel sleepy. Mathematics or the science subjects which need full attention is best suited for the morning session before lunch.

Chapter 8

UPLIFTING THE SPIRIT THROUGH EDUCATION

$\mathcal{E}$very parent wishes that their children receive good education and grow up with certain values in their life. All parents want their children to be happy and prosperous. Prosperity is desired because they want their children to be happy and if they are not prosperous they will not be happy. But in this process, it seems, the vital link to happiness is being broken somewhere. What a beautiful smile a baby or a child has! They have such joy and friendliness. But by the time the same child grows up and moves to school and college that joy, their innocence and beauty is lost. We really need to see if there is some way we can maintain these qualities in spite of children growing older. If we can achieve this then we have done something marvellous. This is because the innocence brings a certain beauty.

An ignorant person can be innocent but that innocence does not have much value. And an intelligent person can be crooked but then his intelligence does not have much value either. What is worth having on this planet is an intelligence that does not destroy innocence. Children in schools and colleges will have just four or five friends. If they do not know how to be friendly with forty or fifty kids in their classrooms, how can they be friendly with six billion people on the planet when they leave their schools and colleges? The basic tendency to make friends has been lost somewhere in the pursuit of selfish education. The sign of success is a smile, friendliness, compassion, and a willingness to serve each other.

It is interesting to see that the structure of an atom and the human consciousness, the mind, is very similar. Protons and neutrons are in the centre, in the nucleus and the negatively charged particles - the electrons, are in orbit in the periphery around the nucleus. So too is the case with human life. All the negativities and vices are only on the periphery. In the core of every being, every person and individual, there is positivity and virtue. We don't have to do anything to bring in virtue. We only have to nourish what is already there. There should be some programs and solutions for the youth to be beaming and radiant. It is very painful to hear about shoot-outs and other crimes taking place in schools and colleges. This was never heard of some decades ago. There was certain respect, honour and dignity attached to education. This has got eroded in the past few years. I think it's high time that we restore those values!

We need a 'broad-minded' education and a 'warm' heart that is the result of that education system. A really well educated person will not look down upon others who are not so educated. He or she will be friendly and compassionate and can be a 'nobody' with everybody. The sense of warmth that spreads in our atmosphere due to this is worth achieving and nourishing in life. People start thinking that only by following a particular religion they can go to heaven; that everybody else will go to hell. They feel that, since they follow a set of rules, the whole world should follow the same and those who do not will go to hell. This kind of wrong understanding about religion has given rise to terrorism in the world today. Terrorism is being bred in schools and colleges. Whether it is leftist or religious terrorism doctrines, they all have their roots in schools and colleges. That's where children start thinking, youths start thinking about what is right and what is wrong and what they should do to make the whole world right. And I have a simple question for them - if they can accept food, music and technology from every part of the world, why they can not accept wisdom too?

In this world only education can bring about open-mindedness (multi-cultural and multi-faith). That should be the goal in bringing up our children. Even if a small part of the planet is left ignorant about this, then it will not be a safe place. So, all the big thinkers and good minds of this society today will have to ponder on it and spread the knowledge of human values, broad mindedness and warm hearts.

Chapter 9

MOTIVATING MISCHIEVOUS STUDENTS

I expect students to be mischievous! When you think of mischief you should start smiling. You should not forget to smile! You must smile everyday, come what may. The success in your life is measured by the smile you have. It's easy to smile when everything is going smooth. But are you able to smile when things are at their worst? Education is something that makes you very strong and vibrant. It makes you smile through tough times and brings in you an air of friendliness despite difficulties. If you are an educated person the smile is your friend. You will ever have an air of friendliness. If you don't have many friends it is because you keep thinking about other people's opinion about you. You need to give everyone the freedom to think and say what they want. The constitution provides freedom of speech to everybody. You should not bother about what others think of you. You should become free from all the buttons which, when pressed, upset you. You should have a personality which is so strong that no one can humiliate you. You should become so powerful and strong that you will not mind if someone criticizes you.

Many students have an attention-deficiency problem. This means that after listening to a lecture for just ten to fifteen minutes they get bored and their attention strays and they lose the thread. This attention and retention problem is something that has really bogged down our youth. To get out of this dilemma some exercises need to be done.

You should have a cordial one-to-one relationship with your teachers. If there is anything that bothers you, you should be able to share it with them. You should have the confidence to do this. You need to do this because there are many things about which you cannot talk to your parents. The alternative is to keep them in your mind and thereby build up the pressure. It is so much better to have confidence in your teachers and share these things with them and take their advice. Do you have teachers who are willing to help you? In this case you may have to take the first step forward and make the connection. In many schools and colleges, students get very depressed, angry, and frustrated. But if they have the right connection with their teachers, then they are helped. Their tensions are eased giving them a sense of relief. Then, the feeling of fun follows. The lightness in their lives returns. All students need some kind of counselling. Teachers can play the additional role of counsellors. Most teachers will love to take care of the students. But the students need to be open with them.

You should aim for an intellect which is free from inhibitions and a mind which is free from confusion. Then, your studies will go on smoothly and effortlessly. If your mind is confused and your intellect has a lot of inhibitions then you won't even retain a fraction of what you study.

Let me summarize:

1. You should make one new friend every day.

2. You should smile more often and through all your problems. You are not machines and do not have to get angry every time someone

insults you, as if you are programmed to do so. You have the freedom to accept or reject a negative remark.

3. You should do something to improve your life.

4. You should have a one-to-one relationship with your teachers and share your thoughts and feelings with them.

Chapter 10

A CONVERSATION WITH TEACHERS

*A*re you all comfortable? Are all of you happy? That is important. You should be happy. Whatever the circumstances, does not matter. You should keep the mind happy. This is the first step in spirituality: keeping the mind happy. We should respect the work we do. You are all teachers. Nobody is respected as much as teachers. What do you all think? Many of you might be thinking, "It would have been nice if I were an engineer." Is this on your minds? How many of you feel this way? Whoever experiences this lack lift your hands, "It would have been nice if I was a doctor or an engineer. It would have been nice if I had got another job. I could not find any job. So, I became a teacher." How many of you feel this way? Lift your hands, I want to see, once again.

Most people think that those who cannot get other lucrative jobs end up becoming teachers. Usually, teachers believe this too. Let's take a look at all the other jobs once. What does an engineer do? Okay, he/she got a degree after five years. What do they do? They go to the factory at 8 o'clock in the morning. They have to get ready by 7 o'clock itself and reach the factory by 8 o'clock. They come back by 8 pm. They have to slog like this six days in a week. Isn't it? Slogging and working with machines, they too become machines. If you see them twenty years later, there will be no difference between them and the machine. They too respond like a machine. If you press a button, the machine works. Similarly, if you say a few not so good words to them, they get angry. If you say a few good words, they laugh. They live like machines. Isn't it?

Then, look at the doctors. Everybody wants to take up the medical profession because they think it is a nice one. What is so great about the doctor's job? Everyday, right from morning they have to be with sick people, isn't it? They have to lead their lives from morning to night in the hospital with sick patients. People keep groaning and moaning on all four sides. They cannot do anything. They cannot save anybody. What do they do? They do some broad and approximate calculations in their mind and give medicines to the patients. The doctors themselves will not exactly know the diagnosis. They do this and that and give medicines. If the patient has good merits, the patient will get alright. Doctors cannot go on leave. They cannot go anywhere. They cannot sleep in peace. Even if it is twelve in the night, patients come home to take them to the hospital. This is their whole life. See, if you need to nurse a patient for a few days how difficult it is for you! A doctor spends all his life listening only to complaints on sickness and disease. Their whole life is like this from morning till evening. Is this an ideal life to lead?

Look at everything from this angle. Look at your life like this. You are with children. You lead your life with growing children. You also get two months of leave. A teacher's job is such that you can lead a peaceful life. So, why consider this as a bad job? Nowadays, everyone gets similar salaries. The salary earned by a professor in a college is equal to the salary earned by a doctor. If doctors are earning more, then they spend accordingly too. What do we get by working so much? Whatever we earn, half of it we spend to cure their diseases.

If we earn thousand rupees we spend five hundred rupees to pay the doctor's fees. Is this a sign of intelligence? Look at everything from this angle. What happens when you look at everything in this manner? You gain confidence in yourself that whatever you are doing is right. You feel firm, you will love your job and will do your job with emotional involvement if you see it from this angle. Then we become 'karma yogis'. If you just come for the heck of it and do something and go away, then it becomes a karma. You should do the same job with love and happiness.

Chapter 11

ADDRESS AT INTEGRATED VALUE EDUCATION CONFERENCE, JUNE 2006

Om namah praNavārthāya shuddha gnāneka mūrtaye
nirmalāya prashāntāya dakshiNāmūrtaye namah

*D*ignitaries on the stage and dear audience, I am getting this message from the garland around your necks. I feel you are giving out a silent message to the crowd saying that education is like fragrance; it cannot be contained. (Applause)

The subtle message that you can derive is that education is like a flower – fresh and alive and has to be handled delicately. It is so delicate. We cannot have value education just for one generation and forget about it. Every generation needs to revive, renew and re-implement it. So, the flowers that you are having on your neck is an indication that we need to handle the situation of our education in a delicate manner.

There is an ancient saying that says :

Swadeshe pūjyate rājā, vidwān sarvatra pūjyate

"A king is honoured in his own country whereas an educationist is honoured everywhere."

Education is universal. It goes beyond the boundaries of nation, religion, race, culture, gender and various other identifications. The knowledge of an educationist is universal. Wherever an educationist is born, he does not belong only to that country but becomes a global person. If an educationist does not become a global person, then he is no educationist at all.

Einstein found out about quantum mechanics, theory of relativity and he was not limited to a country or a place. He crossed the boundaries of identities and became global. This vision we need to create in our children. Today, one of the main problems in the world is identification. Children have been given a particular set of ideas and have not been made to open up to new ideas, not open to the rest of the world. With this they grow up thinking only they are correct, only they are right.

How do we integrate these values into one's life? When I say one's life, it means professional, personal, social and spiritual. This is what we need to ponder upon.

First, we need to discuss the present scenario. The present scenario has lots of difficulties. Education is not just stuffing our kids with useful information. It is to make them beautiful citizens of the planet. A recent research says that a child smiles a lot, about 400 times a day. When it becomes an adolescent, it smiles only 17 times. And once an adult, he/she stops smiling. Is this what we want to achieve? A child, a beautiful flower of this creation is sent to school and by the time he comes out of college, he has a stern and an aggressive face, a stern look, a dejected outlook towards life. We need to seriously think about it. Should education not make an individual much happier? We need to seriously ponder on it.

So, acknowledge the present scenario. The present scenario has lots of dropouts in schools and colleges. The dropout rate is alarming. In Washington DC alone the dropout rate is 50%. Of course, in many countries, this dropout rate we can not even count because children don't go to school at all! There is no question of dropping out. In third world countries, the rate of illiteracy is so high because people don't go to school in the first place. When the child starts crying, the mother says, "Never mind, don't go to school. Go rear the sheep and cattle."

Why is the school dropout rate so high? We need to ponder. Maybe the education system is so.

Chapter12

ANCIENTLY INNOVATIVE

$\mathcal{S}$ystems of education definitely need to improve. A total revolution is needed in the field of education. Today you don't need to memorize by heart the multiplication tables. If the same method of education is followed in our schools and colleges, it is a waste of time. We spend hours and hours learning by rote — rehearsing the Iliads and Shakespeares. This is outdated English and this is thrust on your children. Understanding Shakespeare by heart and knowing it by memory is a big drain of the brain. By following this old methodology of education, this country is wasting all the intellectual capacity and potential.

In this computer age, one can know all about history on just a click. Children spend hours and hours learning when the Mutiny happened, when Macaulay came to India and what reforms he carried out. Obsolete principles, theories, systems of education and methodologies of transmitting knowledge need to undergo a change.

By the time a child comes to college, he or she is already worn out with so much pressure. He carries books on his back -- huge loads of books on irrelevant subjects, totally irrelevant to them. This system needs to undergo a change and we need to harness a child's capacity to digest more, understand more.

A good system of education must instill self-esteem and creativity, and stop copying from others. We need to have self-esteem and appreciate what we have, what we can do. If you take confidence away from a person, there is nothing he or she can do. We have to instill confidence in education, broaden the vision and deepen the roots. The education system shouldn't make people fanatics. People become such narrow-minded fanatics because they glorify the past all the time. Religious fundamentalism is because people glorify only the past. And on the other hand, communism promises you a golden future and says the past is all rubbish. I feel both of them are not right.

In today's education system, there is either communalism or communism. Both are hampering the growth of science. The scientific mind needs to be free from inhibition. The right education must harness a mind that is free, not obsessed with anything and neither angry about the past nor worrying about the future.

The need of the hour is for a system of education where the roots are deep and there are fresh shoots on the tree - a combination of new and ancient.

Sadly, we have not done anything to increase the capacity of our consciousness. At the same time there is a bombardment of information from audio-visual media, movies and video games. This puts such a pressure on one's mind. It would only turn children schizophrenic and attention deficiency syndrome will come up, because their brains cannot digest the information and reproduce it.

The methodology of education needs to change to eliminate a lot of the unwanted information. Creative methods of teaching will help children build their personalities. Creative sports and ancient techniques such as *Avadhanam*, meditation, *yoga* and *pranayams* will go a long way. Dance and music should also be introduced. Service is another good part of education; go and do some service in some place; that is good education. All facets of human life should be attended to and we can start that from a very young age. The key is to harness the ancient and be innovative with the modern.

Chapter 13

THE LARGER PICTURE

$\mathcal{T}$his interview appeared in the Times of India, Bangalore Edition, August 22, 2008

Question: Do you think volunteering and community service by individuals can make a difference in education for children who have no access to formal schooling?

Sri Sri: Volunteering is not an alternative to formal schooling. A formal school education is essential and we must focus on it. In this curriculum, we must have volunteer activities for kids. We do have the National Service Scheme (NSS) system, but it comes much later, at the college level. There should be some service activity which must be introduced at the primary level itself, where children are asked to distribute things etc.

Question: How can the problem of lack of education in rural areas, stemming from a lack of infrastructure, teachers and social conditioning, be countered?

Sri Sri: If all corporate houses adopt a few villages and a few districts in the country, this can be taken care of. There are 612 districts in the country and thousands of corporate houses. If NGOs, government, and corporate houses can work together, I think the goal is not very far from being achieved.

Question: Do you think our education system's methodologies need to be reviewed?
Sri Sri: Definitely. Children are asked to carry a whole load of books on their backs. So many children have a backache by 16, they can't do anything else because their back hurts. We need to bring about a revolution in the education system, where a child learns with his own aptitude. We need to come up with innovative learning methods and not just learn by heart poems in a foreign language. When we were kids, we were taught Shakespeare's verses. It is simply not necessary. Memorizing is such a load. Instead, we must give them an education which uses the right brain and left brain, like music and logic; relaxation, some *yoga*; give them proper food. All this will enable a child to learn better and learn more than you expect them to.

Question: How can attitudes be changed in rural areas towards education of the girl child?
Sri Sri: Through awareness campaigns. Kerala has 100% literacy. Karnataka is moving towards that. Tamil Nadu has high literacy. We need a joint effort of religious institutions, NGOs and the government. Religion can help in a big way. People are religious, women are religious. If religious heads emphasize that every child should be educated, why wouldn't a woman herself send her daughter to school? If every priest in the village says the people must send the girl child to school, his word will be honoured.

Question: One of the primary problems in government schools is absenteeism, both among teachers as well as students. What is the solution to ensure attendance?
Sri Sri: Learning has to be made more fun. Then schools will be able to hold or draw children. In some NGO schools, including Art of Living

schools, the children want to come to school even during holidays. That is because teachers have the attitude of caring for children, they take personal care of them. Teachers and principals must create such an atmosphere in schools.

Question: The Education Bill which will promise universal primary education is expected to be presented in Parliament. How important will this be in ensuring a fundamental right to education? What role should the government play in improving education infrastructure?

Sri Sri: Many times we see that policy makers in education have prejudices. Even among historians, there are left and right wing historians. A prejudice-free mind is absolutely essential for policy makers. We must have a balanced outlook.

We also need to be contemporary. Some policy makers do not even know how to operate a computer. They are two generations behind. They have lost touch with the mental state of students in schools and colleges.

A good teacher is one who can recognize where a child is and where he must reach. Only when you understand the difficulties or challenges of a student, you can become a good teacher or a good policy maker. We need to have interaction, brain storming. So often policy makers are not in touch with the ground reality. We need to keep having seminars, so that teachers and policy makers can update their knowledge. It is appalling to know that 40% of teachers are depressed. When teachers are depressed, what can they transmit to children? That's why children don't want to be in school, they want to run away from school.

Policy makers must create learning systems for the teachers. One, through continuing education programmes; two, by deleting unwanted things from the books that are burden for a child's mind. A child who has studied high school and college, goes back home in the village and does not know how to repair a pump. They don't know anything about agriculture. They don't know how to fix a radio or a bulb. That is, students can't earn a living with what they have studied. If education cannot help you earn your bread, we have to reframe education. After school, simple skills must be taught, especially in rural areas. Some knowledge of agriculture is a must.

Question: There has been talk of making education more inclusive by inviting public schools to open up their premises to accommodate second and third shifts after traditional school hours for the education of underprivileged children. Do you think that can be an effective strategy?
Sri Sri: I think it's good. It will go a long way in bridging the urban – rural divide, and the rich – poor divide. Quality education can be given to such children; not just in cities, even in semi – urban areas. Buses must fetch children from the remote places. Taking a ride in a bus everyday can motivate children to go to school. Adult literacy is also important. These institutions can play a major role in this.

Question: Broadly speaking, what measures do you think are required to achieve the Millennium Development Goal of Education for all?
Sri Sri: Four institutions are needed to be able to achieve the Millennium Development Goals. The government's role is essential. There must be a greater budget allocated to education. Not for just opening universities and having more unemployment, but for giving primary education at the lowest cost, or free of cost.

Today, in India, 51% of post graduates and 39% graduates are unemployed. This is appalling. Why would you want your son or daughter to spend so much time and so many years to become unemployed? When they are unemployed, crime increases. Therefore, a good primary education is a must. Religious and spiritual institutions must join hands in this. Those with a spiritual education will not get involved in criminal activities. So, spiritual institutions also have a role. The third is NGOs, as they have creative ideas, plans and proposals. If they implement these in their schools, such schools excel. The fourth is corporate houses. If all these four sectors come together, the MDG will not be a dream, but achieved in a couple of years.

Question: More than 90,000 people have responded to Teach India's call for volunteers. What message would you like to give them and NGOs involved in education?
Sri Sri: Work together. Intellectuals often do not come together. Each one thinks he knows best. There is no team spirit. But they must come together with one goal – in bringing quality education for all. If this can be done, we can achieve it.

For this, we need a violence – free environment. Volunteers must be healthy, free from prejudices; with a little tinge of spirituality – it can bring about so much joy in those who want to work. If working is an expression of your joy, you will spread that happiness all around. You will create the sort of education that you are aspiring for.

Chapter 14

THE CHILD, SCHOOL AND SOCIETY

This talk was Guruji's address to school teachers and principals on "Education for responsibility" – the child, school and society on 17.11.2004, Bangalore

You know, the best form of teaching would be through dialogues. In a dialogue you discuss various view points. A single view point cannot make a dialogue. Contradictory view points alone can make a dialogue. There is an old proverb in Sanskrit which says, "*Vade Vade Jāyate tattva bodhāha.*" It is through discussion that we arrive at the truth. By arguments the cream of knowledge comes up; argument is not for an argument's sake. You have to argue for *tattva jnāna* or the highest knowledge. So, we will keep this session as one such argument. So, I will ask you tough questions and you will all ask me even tougher ones and let us see what comes out of this.

Usually, people argue when they are hot headed or when they lose their temper. Such arguments are worth nothing. They lead you into war and destruction. Let us see what an argument with a cool state of mind or a pleasant state of mind can bring about. We are all in a cool state of mind now. So, we can start an argument.

The child, the school and the society - these are the three tiers. First, the child, then, the school and then the society. Are they all in harmony? Is the child in harmony with the school and is the school in harmony with the society? If they are not in harmony, if they are in disharmony, is the disharmony leading to more creativity and development or is it leading one towards destruction?

Too much harmony is sometimes too static. It does not bring about any dynamism, any improvement. You will find this in the corporate sectors and the factory areas where all the employees live comfortably. They have a home, they have a school, they have everything. People lack enthusiasm, people lack initiative. People lack life there. It is almost mechanical there because everyone knows what they have to do. Their roles are defined. Everyone has their own jurisdictions. Everything is set. Have you seen this? You go to a factory, the finance department will do finance; purchasing will only be by the purchase department; publicity will only be by the publicity department. They do all their functions but, it is like almost dead energy there. Everything stands still. It is static. Wherever there is uncertainty, I tell you, there is more creativity. It is sometimes security which brings lethargy and slows down the process of creativity. So this is one argument. You put forth another argument, then we will see what we can do.

Question: What about trust? Is not uncertainty dangerous?
Sri Sri : If there is trust then there is no uncertainty. If the uncertainty goes to such an extent that you are not even certain about yourself, then you are in complete destruction. Anything in excess is bad. When uncertainty goes beyond a certain limit, then it can create self doubt.

Question: What to do if it is difficult to trust people sometimes?
Sri Sri: Many times you can trust situations but, you cannot trust people. Why people? You cannot trust your own mind. Your choices change so often. The whole world is all about uncertainty. So, what

do you do? Are you ready to take it as a challenge? Are you ready to take a risk, take a jump, take a lead? Then you succeed. Every uncertain situation brings a challenge. That challenge is the mother of creativity. Now, this situation is time bound. But if the uncertainty extends to an unlimited time or if it is a continuous process, then what happens? We will have to wait and see. It can lead you to two situations. One, it will bring a person to more contentedness. More spiritual awakening can happen or, on the other hand, the person can become cynical or shut down the heart. An eye-opening towards something that is beyond reason, a certain trust in the divine order dawns or the person becomes cynical.

The Child

Today, the lack of spiritual or ethical education has led our students towards suicidal tendencies on one hand or naxalite tendencies on the other. Naxalite and violent tendencies have risen in them. To bring them on the middle path, what is needed is an education about themselves - about their mind, their breath, their concepts, about their reality. That is essential. Don't you think so?

The School

Now we come to the school. The responsibility of the school is to educate a child and at the same time, not to vanquish all the virtues that a child is born with. A child is born with virtues and a school should see that it protects their virtues, that innocence, the sense of belongingness, love and trust which every child is born with. Often in the education system, the school only caters as an information bureau, but not as a personality building centre. Most schools can produce great computers but only a few good human beings. Do you agree with me?

We have brilliant students. They have information about the world. Just by one question they can answer all the information that is needed. But, are they good human beings? Do they know how to behave well? Are they cultured, civilized, compassionate human beings? This is a question that every school and every teacher should ask.

The Society

We have to take care of this. This is very important. In the school you teach them moral education. But, just outside the school, outside the compound of the school if there is pornography, if there is alcohol, if there are drugs being sold, you are not safe. Whatever you did in the school is not going to flourish. The school is also responsible for the environment in the society. School teachers, headmasters and headmistresses are the guiding force. They have to ensure that such activities do not pop up in the society. They need to bring about co-operation and advise the relevant authorities against destructive social environment.

You must have heard that school education is good in America. But, the children go out and watch television and all the violence and crime and they come with guns and shoot all the kids in the classroom. Classroom violence! Even in India this has happened at a couple of places! This is because the society is responsible for the violence in the school. No teacher will teach a kid to take a gun and shoot other kids. Why do children commit such crimes? It is because the school has remained isolated in the society. Isolation will not help. It will create more tension, more problems. So, it is the responsibility of the school teachers to continuously have a dialogue with the parents and with other agencies in the society. I would say that the Teachers' Association should have a big say in the censorship of movies. A school teacher representative should be a part of the censorship board because they know what type of movies children should not be exposed to. Such a composite culture needs to be developed between the school, the society and the child. Only then you can really create responsible citizens in the society. Today, the teachers are so desperate in one of the states in India, doctors are on strike. Nobody feels safe anymore. This type of uncertainty is not what we want.

Question: Does it not affect our children if the curriculum is changed with the change of political parties?

Sri Sri: You are correct. This concern needs to be addressed. Academics needs to be given preference. No caste, community or religion should come as a barrier there. I think that it is not a healthy attitude. A child should be taught human values. There should be broad-mindedness. A child should know a little about all the cultures and religions of the world. If they are exposed to diversity from childhood, they will not turn out to be fanatics. Children turn fanatic in some countries because they are not exposed to various cultures and religions in the society. You need to create a broad outlook and deep roots.

Question: Guruji, I am a teacher and already elderly. How can I press for all these reforms now?

Sri Sri: Why cannot you press, tell me? There can be only three reasons. Number one is that you do not have the time. Second one is that you feel that you will not be heard by the people. And third you think that it is practically impossible. Which of these is your reason? If you think that it is practically impossible, if you have a *dhārana* (a strong thought about it), then begin to think that it is possible. Second, if you think that you will not be heard, never mind. You keep shouting. Somebody will hear. If you think that it is time which is constraining you, I tell you, it may just be an oversight on your part. A peon in a school or a bank has 24 hours. He complains, that he has no time. A Prime Minister too says the same thing, "I have no time." Both of them have 24 hours and look at the magnitude of the difference in work they both do.

I will tell you an example of Swami Prabhupad. Swami Prabhupad, at the age of 72, went on a ship from Calcutta. He boarded a ship and went to America to introduce the knowledge of the *Bhagavat*. At that age, with little knowledge of English! He even had a heart attack on the way. You should read about such inspiring stories, about people, who at the fag end of their lives achieved a great deal of success. So, we simply need to have that confidence. Like Anna Hazare, he was a simple army soldier. When he came out of the army, he wanted to free the society from corruption and he worked for it. He is seventy plus something now and if he goes on a fast now, there are one and a half lakh people who also sit on fast with him. There is not a single officer who can go against him. If there is any corrupt official, he will sit on a fast and he has one and a half lakh people fasting with him. The officer has to be either shifted somewhere else or has to correct himself. I always say that the reformer can never be a ruler and a ruler can never be a reformer. So, all the teachers can definitely be reformers. Do you get this?

Question: Is creativity greater in security or in insecurity ?
Sri Sri: This is an enigma. If insecurity alone is the cause of creativity, then Lebanon, Sudan and Ethiopia should have been the most creative regions of the world. That is not so. If security alone is the cause of creativity, then even that is not so because in Finland, Norway and Denmark there is total security. The government takes care of everything for everybody. Whether you work or not, you are paid, you have money, you have medical coverage. Everything is provided. You do not find them creative either. So, where is creativity ? This you have to search. It is somewhere in between, you need to be great to find out where it is great.

Question: What should the teacher do to bring down violence in the Society?
Sri Sri: I think teachers will have to wake up. I just heard an instance

yesterday that a doctor in Bihar was asked by an extortionist to pay one lakh rupees. As he was the personal doctor of the minister, he said, "I am not going to pay you any money." So, he went up to the minister to complain and he found that the extortionist was sitting next to the minister. The minister tells the extortionist, "Why do you trouble my doctor?" He turns to the doctor and says, "Anyway, do some bargain. Give him 50% instead." The doctor was shocked. Why? This is because the teachers only remain as information instruments, who merely pass on the information and do not play the role of a mentors. They allow people to go out of school without taking care of their moral and ethical values and growth of their inner self. Other states have not yet reached that level of misgovernance and we should not let it happen.

You will be surprised to see that many professors or teachers who have stood for Naxalism and who are the fathers of Naxalism in the country. The teachers were themselves not practicing nonviolence. They induced hatred into these young minds in the colleges and well educated youths today have become naxalites. A teacher in Delhi University is teaching in this manner, "Why do you show the flame to God in temples? It is because the *adimanava* or the primitive man was threatening God with *agarbati* (incense stick), 'You better take care of my desire. Otherwise, see what I have in my mind'. If God did not get scared by *agarbati*, he would take camphor and go round the God and say, 'I will burn you if you do not take care of me'. This is what the primitive man would do to get his wish fulfilled." This is what the teacher is teaching children! How can the student not become violent? I think we need to bring up the principle of nonviolence, humanity, compassion and love. They all have this responsibility.

Chapter 15

YOUR QUESTIONS ANSWERED

QUESTIONS FROM PARENTS

Question: Dear Guruji, please talk on parenting.

Sri Sri: Your evolution is very fast when you are a parent. You are very keen and on your toes all the time like the security guard of a VIP. You are only worried about external things. When you are calm and serene, the children catch on to that. Sometimes children also talk like fifty-year olds. They are like parrots. A couple should not quarrel or do anything that is not good before their children. A sense of giving should be developed in them. They should be endowed with the seed of spirituality.

Question: What is your advice to parents?

Sri Sri: When you ride a horse, you must move with it. You have to rock with its motion otherwise your back will hurt. It is the same with kids. Parents have to rock and swing with them - know them and gently guide them. Sometimes you need to tighten the reins and sometimes you must loosen them. Sometimes you need to put your foot down and, at other times, give them freedom.

Question: What is the most valuable thing you can do to your children? Love?

Sri Sri: Love is always there. You can't help but love your children. What you need to do is to educate them in human values and make them kind and strong. Some children are kind but they can be easily hurt. They get offended easily and become miserable. And some are very strong but they are not kind. It is a challenge to make your children strong as well as kind. Sometimes you have to scold them. You should not bring them up in a goody-goody way all the time. If they are used to your getting angry with them, then they will not get upset if someone else gets angry at them in the future. Otherwise, they may become very fragile, delicate and vulnerable. So, sometimes you have to scold them and put them on the right path.

Question: How can parents raise responsible children and make the experience joyful for both?

Sri Sri: Children should be taught to make one new friend each day. They should not be allowed to play violent video games. Then, there is 'ART Excel' - All Round Training in Excellence. Children really enjoy this program as they learn the essential points through games. In Europe it is known as NAP - Non-Aggression Program. After doing this program, even very aggressive children become happy and friendly. We conduct a program called "Know Your Child" for parents. Life is a gift to you; a very charming gift. But you seldom open it. It's all about opening yourselves, being open. Life is gift-wrapped in golden paper which is waiting for each one of you to unwrap it. You need to be in an informal atmosphere to know yourself and acquire deep wisdom. Formal atmosphere is not conducive for knowledge.

Most of the time, you do not actually mean the pleasantries that you exchange with people. Most of your pleasantries and conversation are on a superficial level; very nearly like an air hostess telling you to have a nice day after a flight! If you are told something similar by your grandmother, it carries energy, vibrations, and presence. When you relate to everybody on a very superficial level all the time then life becomes dry and the world dull. It is all just about "Hi" or "Hello." In the coming decades, the biggest challenge in the world will be mental depression. This can be countered by belongingness which can create a better atmosphere and environment around. It depends on you to create that environment. Feeling at home wherever you are and whoever you are with, is the true evolution of human beings. For this to happen, you need to look within yourself; just a glance to know what is bothering you and what is restraining your capacity to connect with everyone around. A baby smiles four hundred times a day, a teenager only smiles seventeen times, and an adult hardly smiles at all. You don't smile from your hearts. This is because of the stress and the tension that you carry in you. Can we be stress-free and have a stress-free society? First we need to have a dream; a vision. And then we need to work towards realizing it.

Question: There is so much competition in society that the kids have no time to relax. There is a fear that they will not fit into the society. How do we handle this situation? What is the *mantra* for excellence?

Sri Sri: You should not push them too much. Teach them to relax. Music, meditation and some games will help.

Question: How to cope with a child's expectation when they compare themselves with others and demand the things that others have?

Sri Sri: You have to tell them that you can only give them so much and not more; that they should not compare themselves with others. But it is important that you don't give them any false hopes. At the same time, you can give them a dream. You can tell them that if they do well in their studies then they will realize their dreams. Here lies the importance of bringing them up with sensitivity and belongingness. If you participate instead of teaching them, they will not even question you. Then they will be sensitive towards you rather than demand of you. Before you become a good father or mother, you need to become a good 'uncle' or 'aunty' - communicate more with your children's friends. They will listen to you. If your children's friends have wrong habits, you can influence them to change. They will listen to you more than to their own parents. Similarly, other parents can take better care of children than their own .

Question: How do we teach our children our culture? They are caught between two cultures. This is difficult for children as well as parents.

Sri Sri: You must hold weekend workshops for them to make them understand. Children may ask what is the point in doing *aarati*? It should be explained to them that it is a prayer to let one's life always be around the Divinity and never move away. And it should be further explained that the touching the eyes with the palms held over the sacred flame of the *aarati* signifies acceptance of the light and the wisdom into one's life. People ask why there are so many Gods and Goddesses in India. It is simple - God loves variety. He did not make one type of vegetable or one type of fruit. The Divine also loves variety and manifests itself in many ways. Why do you want to put the Divine in one uniform? He can choose any number of garments and costumes! You should explain this to your child. We take *teertha* because it gives peace and calmness to our minds and generates love. What is *prasāda*? It gives *prasannatā* - blissful happiness.

Why do we wear a *bindi* (the dot on the forehead)? It stimulates the pituitary gland. Usually, when we think, we put our fingers on our forehead, and when we make a mistake we touch the back of the head! When you stimulate the pituitary gland all glands in the body get stimulated. Even men wear *tilak* of sandalwood paste, etc. Women are more emotional. So, to control the emotions, the *bindi* was insisted upon in the earlier days. Our alertness also increases if we apply sandalwood paste. All this has been scientifically researched. In Karnataka we have a custom of mirror and *kalasha* during marriage. People carry the mirror and *kalasha* (pot full of water with coconut and leaves on top) at the entrance of the marriage party. Whenever they come across someone the mirror is shown. When a person sees his or her own reflection in the mirror, there is a tendency to smile. So, when it is shown to an angry person the anger evaporates. This is because everybody likes to see themselves happy. That is why the mirror is shown to all the invites. It is believed that by this all the distortions like anger, greed, jealousy, etc in the atmosphere are removed. And then the *kalasha* follows. It signifies fullness in a person. The mirror removes distortions and then the fullness is revealed!

QUESTIONS FROM TEACHERS

Question: Can motivation be taught?
Sri Sri: Motivation is something that is 'injected' from outside. And inspiration comes from inside. You can motivate a person, but the motivation will be short-lived. Maybe you give some prize but that motivation does not last long. Inspiration can last for the whole life.

Question: What is the most important aspect for the students to focus on when you wish to motivate them?
Sri Sri: You should encourage them to have dreams. You should tell them stories that inspire them and give them ideals to strive for and moral values to live by. When they have an ideal before them, they will have a role model. There is an advantage and a disadvantage to this. Sometimes, when a person idealizes someone, they might think it is not possible to achieve that level of accomplishment themselves. They think it is too difficult or they think they do not possess the same abilities. This is an excuse to shy away from working toward that ideal. Worship helps overcome this. In this sense, worship means

idealizing with a feeling of gratitude. It is expressing gratitude. It is a wonderful quality that enriches you and shows an expanded awareness of your own consciousness. Just idealizing can take you away from reality and having no ideal can make you depressed and leave you groping in darkness. Kids in schools and colleges today are often depressed because they have no ideals; no worthwhile role models. If you can't identify an ideal, you can't move forward. The kids don't see their parents and other elders as having qualities worth idealizing. Just as a river needs a direction to flow, so too does life need a direction to move. Children and young adults look for someone to idealize and often look to celebrities (rock stars, movie stars, sports stars, etc). They find their role models on MTV. Unless you have some ideal to look up to, life does not seem to move forward. And this is natural. And there will be both, advantages and disadvantages.

Teachers can be a living example for their students. It is not that teachers should expect students to idealize them! People who are worth idealizing do not care whether others idealize them or not. Everyone needs to see that you not only teach human values but also live by them. It is better for the children to have a role model or a goal because then the worshipping quality can dawn in them.

Worship means feeling gratitude, love, confidence and trust. And that deep feeling wants an expression. It is good to express gratitude. Without gratitude and respect for each other, this world will not be a nice place to live in. We need to bring it out in people - worshipfulness toward each other and towards everyone. The idea of worship has been discouraged for many years in the West. This has also been spreading to the East. Instead of stopping worshipping, we need to encourage it. Since we have stopped adoring and respecting people, it has led to more violence in our societies. Just imagine if the people who move around using guns had some respect and worshipfulness in them and some regard for the people around then they would be different all together! It does not matter what people choose to worship - trees, a cross, this person or that symbol. It does not matter. The feeling of worshipfulness is what is essential. It doesn't even matter if it is a pop star! But that emotion has to rise genuinely from within. That is important. You should not discourage people from idealizing, respecting, and adoring others. In the East, the tradition is for the children to worship their mothers everyday. Then, the father is worshiped, then the Guru and then any guest in the house. The children may have arguments with their parents during the day but every morning they have to make up because they have to bow down to them in worshipfulness to begin the new day. If they fight again, at least they are starting afresh!

Life has many different colours. We have to accept life with all its flavours and colours. Today we need to educate people to adore, worship and appreciate more. You should not be paranoid about worship, gratitude, love and appreciation. Instead, you should be paranoid about violence, arrogance, abusive language, anger and frustration around you.

Question: Nowadays principals and college teachers say that teaching is a business and students are customers. What is the right approach?
Sri Sri: We have not given enough respect to business. Anything that is a business is looked down upon. We deplore spirituality being made into a business; so too, education and politics. It is as if business is something terrible that nobody should touch. This attitude has taken a big toll in our society, country and civilization. With very little resources Portugal, a tiny country captured a big chunk of South America. Portugal is not even the size of Maharashtra! Perhaps it is the size of Kerala. People from this country went forth and captured Brazil. Spain, perhaps the size of Madhya Pradesh, captured the

rest of South America and Central America. This is because they respected business.

In India there is a tendency to put down business as if it is a crime. Business should never be seen as a crime. It should be given its due respect and position. This country has not captured any other country, neither in war nor in trade. Of course, wisdom has travelled to the north, the east, the Far East, etc. People have always come here and taken things which they sold elsewhere. Our merchants did not go far and wide. We have never taken our culture out anywhere. But now we have to take a different approach.

Business should be respected as well. You should also have a business-like mind if you want to run an educational institution. Otherwise, it cannot develop or even survive. At the same time human values should not be lost. The balance between business and human values are to be maintained in the educational field. You have to honour your customers the way you honour God. Then, you are a genuine businessman. So, it does not matter if the Principals think children or students are customers. But they should know that the customer is God. If the customer becomes God to them then it does not matter. They can think it as a business.

Question: Where did we learn to be afraid of making mistakes?
Sri Sri: There are many people who have no fear of making mistakes. Many students who have no fear drop out of school and are involved in violence. Recent statistics show that as many as thirty percent of the children in North America are resorting to some form of violence. This is a very big number. They resort to violence because they are not afraid of making mistakes. There must also be another thirty percent who are afraid to make mistakes. They will not be interested in taking risks and will shy away. Ideally we need to maintain a balance.

We are afraid of making mistakes because of the consequences. We think that we will be punished or that the consequences will be very bad. Often those who have been punished several times are no longer afraid of the consequences. You cannot totally eliminate fear, nor should we. Fear is like salt in food. It keeps people on their toes. It keeps their feet on the ground. But fear is essential only to some degree. If there is too much salt then the food will not be edible. And, at the same time, you cannot eat food which has no salt in it.

A little bit of fear is essential in the process of growth; nature has built you like that. You drive on a particular side of the road because of the fear of having an accident. You walk on the sidewalk and only drive on through a signal when it turns green. This happens due to fear. If you are totally without fear then you will violate all the laws. Laws are always followed due to fear and it is good. But if there is too much fear, it cannot be helpful. You need to have the right amount of fear like salt in food.

Question: When I teach my students I'm mostly dealing with their awful behaviour towards each other. They tell me it is acceptable. But I find it to be very degrading and the language very foul.
Sri Sri: If such children are involved in more physical activity or exercise, their rage or abuse will lessen. Generally, children who are involved in a lot of physical education and who do a lot of physical activity are not very abusive verbally. The problem is with children who play soft games in which much physical work is not required. They are more abusive. When they show disrespect to you and are abusive, they can be mimicked. Then they can be told that, that is how they look and sound like and can be asked if it looks good. They will not like their image and will stop. You can mimic them or create a sense of fun out of their abuse and get everyone laughing. Then the whole thing becomes a game, a play or joke instead of getting tense and unpleasant. Then, immediately you have to put

a stop to it. Now you will have a more effective way to stop their abuse because the group will back you. Otherwise, if you just scold the mischief-maker, there is a likelihood of the group backing him. With a sense of humour you can change the atmosphere to your favour. All the students will be with you because they are all united in laughter. This is a skill in handling a class. Humour is the lever that can transform disrespect into respect. Handing out advice or wisdom will not work.

Sometimes there are some very thick-skinned students with whom humour will not work. Then, you must act and not react. Silence can work along with a little indifference. You should ignore them. And if that does not work, then you can raise your voice. But the more centered you remain the less likely it is that you will have to go beyond a point of indifference.

Question: How to motivate students who are not interested in studies and have an uneducated parental background?

Sri Sri: You should make education more audio visual - more interesting and captivating. If you just talk and talk history in the class, the students will fall asleep. But if the same thing is shown to them audio-visually, then there will show much more interest. Israelis are very good at this. In Jerusalem recently, they insisted that I see a simulator where you are taken through their history in just twenty minutes - from the times of Moses to the current period. You feel as though you are present in the scenes you are seeing. Seeing such a display, a student can 'experience' history rather than read a book trying to remember all the dates which is so irrelevant for today's life and is such a load on his mind. Then, he will remember everything well. The way history, geography, biology, chemistry, physics, etc are taught can be upgraded with the use of computers. Today, we have the amenities to do this. Everything today can be made more interactive. This will make a big difference.

Question: What do you do when children has behaviour problems and the other children avoid them?

Sri Sri: You should make all the children sit in a circle and put the child with the problem in the middle and have everyone shake hands with him or her. You can make them dance with the child or write a nice card for him/her. You may consult some of them and ask them what can be done to help the child. You can say that the child doesn't feel good about being avoided. This will bring compassion in them. You can ask them if they will do you a favour and talk to the child or give him/her a flower or something. This will give them a feeling of pride. And they will help the child who is being avoided. The child who needs help may not be willing to listen to the teacher, but can take advice from one of his friends. The friend, who is teaching or telling the child something, also feels that he is important because he is doing an important job. The process is elevating for both the child who is helping and the one needing help. This is like peer tutoring - not just in lessons but also in behaviour. The current generation needs to culture more helpfulness. The children of today will create the society of tomorrow. Teaching them human values should not just be our desire, it should be our obligation.

Society today has been planting the seeds of violence in children. Most of their toys and games involve violence and, therefore, are very ugly. This violence gets ingrained in their system. Children are not feeling the refined qualities within themselves. Television too has made children very insensitive to violence. The movies, even the cartoons are violent. This violence is stored in the child's conscious and subconscious mind. There is nothing shown about uniting and bringing together. It is not that there cannot be any banging and breaking, but having too much of it influences the mind and creates a subtle unconscious tension. And, as they grow up to be ten or fifteen years old, this tension will be visible on their faces. They will not be like bubbles of joy and bliss which they actually are. They will seem to be cramped up inside.

We have to do something to create an atmosphere for positive growth. The teaching of nonviolence is totally absent in our schools and colleges. The children should be told stories of Jesus or Buddha; stories of compassion and service. These will help to develop the positivity in them. Children see life and emotions in every animal. For them the elephant talks; so does the bear, the bees and all other creatures! Recognizing life is inborn in them. Any child anywhere in the world sees life and emotions in all the species. This is natural. When we were children we were told that if we killed a lizard, we would be born as one. Killing was a sensitive issue. If one cut down a tree, one had to plant five trees in its place. If one did not, then there would be problems in life. Such belief systems were there.

The classroom can be a very good place to instill these values. It is also a very significant place because they spend so much of their time there. The teachers should be telling them inspiring stories about nonviolence and telling them that violence is a shame. They should be told that compassion is a sign of dignity. This can really bring about a change. You need to create a dislike for violence in them by bringing out more positive and inspiring human values. If you teach them to be sensitive to a butterfly, their respect for all life will grow. They should be given a broad vision of sharing. They should be encouraged to share whatever they have with everybody. Very young children often have a tendency to hold onto things. They should be trained even when they are young to have a habit of sharing. They could, for example, be given a box of candy and asked to distribute it to everyone. Sharing is a natural tendency. We have to see that it is cultured and maintained.

Question: I work in a rotating situation and see the same children once each weekday for one hour. It is difficult to establish a connection because of the time lapse between classes.
Sri Sri: It is not the length of time but the quality of time that matters. Sometimes I meet my students for just two days in a year and that is

enough. You should establish a personal connection with them, give each some work or exercises to do, and attend to that the next time they come. As teachers, you have to tell them about their mistakes. And yet not make them feel guilty about them. If you make them feel guilty, they will become your enemies (at least they will think that you are their enemy). At the same time you have to make them aware of their mistakes. This is really a big skill and creates the sense of belongingness. When you have a sense of belongingness, you will be able to tell them anything without creating a sense of guilt in them. There will be love in your relationship.

Normally, you will want to tell people about their mistakes because you love them. You don't do this to strangers on the street. You don't care enough for them to tell them about their mistakes or you don't feel any love for them. You want to point out someone's mistake because you feel for them and want to help them. If they do not understand it, you have to say it in such a manner that they can and yet you do not feel guilty doing so.

Question: Character is said to be an important aspect in the student's life. Why?
Sri Sri: That is because, whatever is learnt now will come in later life. That is why. Student life is the foundation. Do you know what happens? Many emotions arise in them. When they are students, then too, at that age many emotions arise. When you give a proper direction to all those emotions, if they are used in a proper manner, then that energy takes up a different direction altogether. Otherwise, that energy gets distorted and bad habits and bad behaviour begins to arise.

Question: What should be the state of mind of the teachers to correct the mistakes committed by adolescents?
Sri Sri: If somebody does a mistake, do not take that into you and brood over it. The moment we know that others have done a mistake,

we get angry and furious. The mistake we do is that, we get angry and we do a bigger mistake. Therefore consider others' mistakes as your own and then advise them. Many a times, our own fingers prick our eyes. Many a times, when we are eating, we tend to bite our own tongue by our own teeth. If you say, "Teeth, how dare you bite the tongue. I will break all of you," and decide to break your own teeth, what is the use? There is a saying - a nose that is chopped off in anger, will it come back once you have become calm? So, when you point out one finger towards others as 'you', three fingers are pointing towards us. (He gesticulates by stretching the index finger). What happens when you do this? If you say, "You are bad", then you are three times more bad. If you say, "You are very good", then you are three times more good. So, do not fold your fingers, rather show all of them. It means that, instead of showing in this manner (instead of pointing out the index finger), show this way (He shows out his stretched palm). There is complete knowledge in this, "You, you".

If some mistake happens through you then you say, "Oh! it just happened. Leave it. Do you think that I did it on purpose? Do you think that I said that on purpose?" You justify yourself. You say "Oh! I just joked about it. Do you think that I said that on purpose?" But if somebody else does a mistake, you say, "They did it on purpose. They have done this out of jealousy. They have done this out of ego." You try to find an intention behind other people's mistakes. We argue and justify that what we have done is the right way. But you say that others have done it on purpose. This is wrong, isn't it? Even if they have done a mistake, understand that they have no awareness, no conscience, no memory, they are in the forgetful state of mind. Then your mind becomes peaceful.

Question: Guruji, there are Indian teachers present here and we, the teachers from Western countries are present here too. Can you guide as to how to bring up children and handle them? Even

though we are all from different countries, we all do encounter some difficulties while bringing up children. Are there any common solutions to overcome these problems?

Sri Sri: If you know how to bring up children, then it means that you have learnt how to ride a horse. You should learn how to ride a horse. How do you ride a horse? The reins are in your hands. Sometimes you let it loose and sometimes you hold it tight. If you hold the reins too tight then the horse will not run forward. If you leave the reins too loose then the horse goes wherever it wants to. It will be like the Mullah Nasruddin story. Have you heard this story? No?

Once Mullah Nasruddin was sitting on a horse. He was riding in the town and was going round and round and round many times in the same place. People who saw this became curious. They all came to the Mullah and asked him, "Why are you riding in one place like this from a long time? Where are you going?" Mullah replied, "How should I know where I am going? You should ask my horse where it is going. My horse is going somewhere and I am just sitting on it. That is all." So, if you are very free with children and are very lenient and let them very loose, once they grow up, they come back and blame you for not disciplining them.

This happens in many homes. Parents are under this feeling that they should not reprimand children at all. If you do that, then they become incapable of taking even small abuses by anybody. It becomes unpalatable to them. They will become incapable of receiving anything from this world. So, sometimes scolding them a little, little squeezing of ears, getting small work done from them will be helpful. But do not do it too much. Use this in a limited manner. After doing this, do not develop a sense of guilt over it. The most difficult thing is that, parents punish their children and feel extremely guilty over it "Oh! poor thing. Small, little one. I should not have done this to the little one. I am a very bad person. I am like that." Stop blaming yourself. Do not do that. Here and there, now and then, it is okay to give them a slap or two. Everything is a way to get work done.

Question: What is your advise to teachers in instilling self-confidence in children?
Sri Sri: Before instilling confidence, it is important to first identify our mistakes. What happens when we find fault in ourselves? Our self-confidence decreases, lessens, this is one. Another thing is that, when the life force (*prana shakti*) in us decreases our bravery decreases too. You should increase your *prana shakti*. Are you getting this? When the *prana shakti* increases, enthusiasm increases too. Self confidence increases too. The mind is happy and pleasant. By instilling confidence, by being happy, we can create a beautiful society. Creation of a beautiful society is in our hands. All of you should get together to do it. Now, all of you have learnt this knowledge. You should inform your friends, neighbours and everyone else about this knowledge. You can all become teachers of this too. Then, you can teach everybody. This is the real training, the real education.

When you do all these practices for a little while, if you meditate for at least 10-15 minutes in a day, the mind becomes firm. Already many of you might be experiencing some changes in you. We spend ten, twelve years to learn alphabets well, to pass school and to get a degree. But we have never spared time to learn about our lives. That is why we have called this program the "Art of living" - the art of living life, learning about life. If we spare 4-5 days in a week for this purpose, we feel very enthusiastic. When we spread this knowledge to everybody and when everybody learns these beautiful principles, then happiness spreads in the society.

See, we require more peace when we are in difficulty in life. When the mind is peaceful, you get proper thoughts. When the mind is disturbed and is in worry, you cannot think properly. So, when you are caught up in a difficult situation, when things are getting worse, do *kriya*. When you meditate then, your mind becomes stable and firm and then begins to think. Then we can take proper decision. This is necessary. Usually what do people think? They think that when everything becomes alright, when we do not have any problems, then we will sit and meditate. It is not like that. We should always meditate.

There are many ways. You can choose any one path. See, if you want to come to Bangalore, you can come from many different places. You can come from Hosur, from Tumkur, from Chitradurga, from Sirigere, from Mysore. You can come to Bangalore from any direction. But what do we get by knowing all these routes? Not necessary. We only need to know how to go forward from whichever place we are in. So, meditate.

Question: Guruji, can we teach *Sudarshan Kriya* to children and from what age?
Sri Sri: It is enough if it is done from 8-10 years of age. Children below that are naturally happy. Their minds are anyway, always happy. All of you present here are above fifteen years, aren't you? (Laughter) Have we spoken on food? Try eating only natural food for one or two days anytime. When you come back again, we will arrange only natural food for you in the ashram. When you eat natural food, the mind and the body becomes so light and you can notice this for yourself. Many times we complain that children are not paying attention to studies, they are not studying well. But the type of food you give them is that way. If you give them heavy food which is also very rich, then that decreases the brain power. So, pay attention to the food you are giving to children.

Question: What do you have to say about today's education system?
Sri Sri: It lacks the essence which can transform students into

responsible human beings. The system has become so mechanical that we are producing human machines out of students. We need to create good personalities out of them. The full development of the human potential is lacking. An all-around development is needed.

Question: You spoke about education and how it can improve the world. Where does God fit into this equation?
Sri Sri: You don't need to fit God anywhere because He is everywhere! Please don't try to find a place for Him. He is omnipresent. If you think you are going to find a place for Him, He will laugh at you. God is the sum of all creation. He is that energy in which we all are. We cannot escape from that energy. God is not someone who is sitting up there in heaven who punishes you when you do something wrong; who is silent when you make a mistake and then comes after you with a stick! This idea of God may be there in books. Yet to me, God is love. And love is permeating this whole creation in every way; in everyone and in everything. When you relax and take your mind inwards, you get this power. It is the basis of creation.

Question: What is *seva* for a student who has lots to study?
Sri Sri: You must study and keep doing a little *seva*. It doesn't matter how much *seva* you do. You should do according to your capacity but should have your heart in it. That would be equal to doing *seva* like anyone with much more time. You should spend quality time with your parents. When you are with them, you should not give them advice, or tell them how they should be; what they should not do. Elderly people just need your company. When you are with them, you should just sing, play, crack jokes or have food with them. You should talk about something that is of interest to them. They are not interested in listening to wisdom or learning any new techniques from you. You should not behave like a teacher. Of course, you may drop a few words of wisdom. But you should check if they are absorbing it. If they are not, just being with them is good enough.

It is not necessary to do only what you like. Know it clearly that the studies are for your own good. Otherwise your life won't go on! You do not brush your teeth every day with love. If you don't like to brush and stop doing it, you will soon lose your teeth. You know that it is good for your health and it is vital. Similarly, there are some things in life that we can't do without. Studying is one of them. Make a habit of reading a scripture the first thing in the morning. Similarly do some *pranayama* for at least ten minutes. Your breath is going in and out, anyway. So, direct it with *pranayama*. If it keeps diseases away, then why not do it? Just as you brush your teeth for dental hygiene, *pranayamas* maintain your mental hygiene! And to have a sharp intellect you need to study, otherwise you will regret it later. You may buy a dress but when you reach home, you may not like it. *Buddhi Yoga* (Intellect *Yoga*) is the best. *Manmaani karna*, ie, following your feelings is inviting misery. *Guru tattva* is *viveka*; discrimination. Does it matter who the Guru is? It is enough to take the knowledge and move forward. Don't worry who the Guru is.

Question: Parents have to undergo much anxiety about their children during examinations. How do you suggest they handle this?
Sri Sri: You need to be calm and, thereby, ensure that the children are calm, too. You should not pressurize them especially when they are about to leave for their examination. You should not make them tensed by asking - if they have studied everything or whether they remember what they had studied. This might cause panic and might adversely affect their performance.

Question: Guruji, how can spirituality be vested in our children and how can it be made part of our educational system?
Sri Sri: We should not make spirituality very serious for the kids. It should be a game that they can enjoy. That's why we have devised the course called 'ART Excel' - 'All Round Training In Excellence'. 'YES'

- 'Youth Empowerment Seminar' is for the young adults. In these courses, the children look at their own inhibitions and barriers - how they arise and how they can be overcome. If someone wears dirty clothes, you may not talk properly with them. It becomes a barrier; an inhibition in the mind. But you will behave well with a saint who has long hair and a beard. And you may hang on to every word of an actress! With them, you may behave differently. It means that we cannot ignore the colour and clothes of a person and look inside him or her. We put up barriers in our mind and we do not look beyond such external manifestations. In our programs we so train the kids that any barriers between the age-groups are removed. Usually, what they share with their class-mates or pears will not be shared with their parents or people of that age-group. The kids thoroughly enjoy 'Art Excel'. and 'YES'. However, I'm little bit hesitant to make it a part of the curriculum. This is because there is no pleasure in anything that is part of the curriculum. Usually children enjoy that which is extra-curricular. (Laughter)

Question: As a teacher, I have been trying to inculcate human values in my children. Whenever I digress from the usual curriculum, I find them getting bored.
Sri Sri: Do you think they are very much interested in their usual curriculum? They are not! You need to make it more interesting. Our experience is the other way around. Whenever something is different from the curriculum, the students get just glued to it and want more. They don't let the teachers end the class. Just anything extra-curricular may not be interesting. But something which is very interesting and interactive and which has games will make them take interest.

Question: Guruji you are amazing. Please advice on how to inculcate spiritualism in kids?
Sri Sri: You need to tell them stories about saints and other mythological stories. They should be made to do some service

activities. They should be inculcated with the habit of 'giving'. Interest in devotional music should be generated in them. The importance of studies in the life of the kids is as important as that of their mothers, fathers or Guru. Parents scold their children when they are lax about their studies because they are worried about their careers. Hence they ask them to study more. The children should not feel scared while studying. They should remember that I am always with them. Education is as important in life as success. If someone cannot concentrate and study alone then he or she can do so with a group of two or three friends. If studies seem a burden then it should be treated as a game. Formulae could be remembered using the names of friends or with stories. This helps to memorize things quickly.

Question: Guruji, I am a teacher and I teach in a high school. Because of some management rules and regulations, sometimes I am bound to give grace marks. This brings guilt in me. I wonder if I am doing justice by promoting undeserving students. On the other hand I am often told that I should not be detaining students because I jeopardize a lot in this process. I am in a dilemma. Please advice.

Sri Sri: First of all, your education system is faulty. Secondly, your examination system is faulty. Sometimes, there are many students who really know the matter well, but are unable to do well because they cannot put it across during the examination. Yet there are also other students who really have no interest in studies and do not do well in the examination as well. Both groups should not be treated in the same way. You should go by your intuition. If deserving students fail but get marks close to the pass mark then you can give them some grace marks to enable them to pass.

Question: How to enhance receptivity?

Sri Sri: If you are listening but the mind is somewhere else then there will be no receptivity. When your mind is clogged with too many ambitions, it will not be interested in anything that is not linked to them. Even if it is related, the mind will go on a day-dreaming trip. It will listen to one sentence and then it will be off on a trip. For e.g. if someone has an ambition of becoming a Chief Minister and he is told that he has all the possibilities of becoming one, then his mind immediately goes on a such a trip. If your mind is stuck with many thoughts then also the perception will be low. Another reason for the decrease in the alertness of the mind is *vata* de-arrangement or *kapha* imbalance. When the mind is bombarded with sensory stimuli then, too, it will not be receptive. Have you observed that, after watching a three-hour movie, if someone tells you something you will not be able to grasp it well? Receptivity can be enhanced by being in silence and doing regular *pranayama*. Having proper food and lesser ambitions will help, too.

Question: When does education become meaningful?
Sri Sri: When an outstanding person is created and when there is enough strength in him then education becomes meaningful. Our lives should be like a coconut. Our involvements should be like the husk. Our body should be like the shell and our mind should be like the white kernel inside. Our heart should be like the sweet water. Our culture and traditions are based on scientific reasoning.

Question: Why do we bother about what other people think about us?
Sri Sri: You should become free from all the buttons that can be pressed to give rise to various emotions and feelings in you. If someone knows exactly what can trigger your anger, then that is the button that can upset you when it is pressed. You should aim to have a personality that is so strong that no one can ever humiliate you. And that can be the outcome of the 'YES' program - 'Youth Empowerment Seminar'. You will become very strong and powerful after attending it and will not mind when you are criticized.

Attention and retention problems are something that has really bogged down our students. To get out of it you need to do some exercises. And the diet needs to be taken care of, too. This is because the food can increase the capacity of your minds. You need to learn a few exercises to really focus. Then, your mind will become as powerful and focused as a laser beam and you will retain anything that you study just once. Your breath can help you achieve this.

You also need to have a cordial relationship with your teachers. If there is anything that bothers you, you should be able share it with them. This is required because there are so many things that you cannot discuss with your parents. And if you cannot discuss them even with your teachers, then the only other way is to keep them in your minds and feel the pressure build up! You may not have teachers who are willing to help. Then, you may have to take the first step forward in making the connection with them. Students get very depressed, angry and frustrated in many schools and colleges. When they are confused they need someone to talk to. And if they have a good connection with their teachers and lecturers then much of this tension can be dissipated by just talking to them about the problems. Then, there will be a feeling of fun and lightness. There is a need for such counselling.

The teachers and lecturers can adopt the role of counsellors, too. But the students need to be open with them. They should aim at having a mind and an intellect which is free from inhibitions and confusions. Then, their studies will be much easier.

Summary:

1. Students should make one new friend every day.

2. They should smile more and through their problems. They are not machines. They need not get angry every time someone insults them.

They should smile when this happens and have the freedom to accept or reject a negative remark.

3. They should do something to improve their lives.

4. They should have a one-to-one relationship with their teachers and lecturers and should share their thoughts and feelings.

Question: You spoke about the importance of a strong personality that is able to withstand humiliation. As a guidance teacher how do I try to strengthen my students' personalities?
Sri Sri: Inhibition holds down a person's personality. And you have to look into it; how they can come out of it. Some boys may be nervous to talk before girls. Some girls may be just as shy and not say a word before boys. So, you need to look into the problem. And students think and worry too much about others' opinions. I feel that they should have the strength to accept criticism. Then, nothing can throw them off balance.

We do many processes in the Youth Empowerment Seminars (YES) to strengthen such areas of the personality. They last for a total of about sixteen hours - a few hours each day.

Question: About five lakh students appear for their standard X and XII exams every year. And because of the tough competition, their families are in tension every year. How to tackle this?
Sri Sri: Let them do some *pranayama, bhastrika, so-ham,* etc.

Question: The Jiddu Krishnamurti style of teaching avoids competition. Do you have any comment?
Sri Sri: All competition should be with yourself - how well you performed the previous year and how well you want to perform in the current year. When you compete with yourself, then you can

perform better. You cannot avoid competition among kids altogether, but you can give a proper direction to the competition.

Question: How do you neutralize the effect of the wrong kind of education, for example the one given in *madrasas*?
Sri Sri: We had done some work in the juvenile detention centres with children who have committed crimes. Children were violent in prisons. We had given them some constructive education and a broad vision about human values.

Question: How to choose a career?
Sri Sri: The choice is yours and the blessing is mine! This is tough at times and it is confusing to choose among the various options available - engineering, medical, architecture, charted accountancy etc. This is all the more confusing if you are proficient in more than one subject. It is good to bake a little bit in that confusion. But it is important that you put in your hundred percent in anything you chose. You may choose medical and, later, feel that you should have opted for engineering, or you may choose engineering and feel, after some time, that you should have gone in for chartered accountancy. These are illusions. Every profession is the same.

QUESTIONS FROM SATSANG

Question: Can you speak about Education?
Sri Sri: Education has five aspects
1. Information - Often we think information is education, but it is only one aspect of education.
2. Concepts - Concepts are the basis for all research. You need to conceive in order to create.
3. Attitude - An integral aspect of education is cultivating the right attitude. Proper attitude at the right time and place determines your actions and behaviour.

4. Imagination - Imagination is essential for creativity and for the arts. But if you get stuck in imagination, you may become psychotic.

5. Freedom - Freedom is your very nature. Joy, generosity and other human values blossom only with freedom. Without freedom, attitudes become stifling, concepts become a burden, information is of no value and imagination becomes stagnant.

Question: I am a student and I am so much impressed with the education system here. Could you please tell me some of the values that I can take back along with me?

Sri Sri: Respect the teachers. There is so much respect for the teachers in the Indian education system. That respect is missing in the western schools and colleges. Also respecting the elders is one of the beautiful cultural identities here.

Question: Can spiritual practices strengthen academic progress?

Sri Sri: Definitely. There has been a research done recently in England that indicate that the children who study Sanskrit excel in mathematics and the linguistic functions of their brain become much better. These children can learn any language easily - from Chinese to English to Russia. Three schools in England have made Sanskrit compulsory. A research was also done to determine why Indians excel in IT. It seems that the brain of an Indian is more suitable for working on a computer. This is because of knowing the Sanskrit language. So, it is good to have your children study Sanskrit. Apart from this, there are a number of researches which show that doing *pranayama* enhances the performance of children. They feel calmer, more attentive, and alert. They are able to perceive and digest better. There are a number of such benefits that have been proved. You can look into the Yes+ website for the benefits that a child gets in the academic field.

Question: Why does everyone not aspire to serve the society in their youth?
Sri Sri: It must be there. There is no heart that does not get affected by the sight of misery. At one time, everyone should desire to do *seva*. We cannot say that we will not do *seva*.

Question: How does a youth handle the ups and downs of life?
Sri Sri: I am a youth myself! Life is a mixture of everything – success and failure. They complement each other. If you fail, then you know the value of success. It is a stepping stone. You need to move forward. Ask yourself what you have learnt from the past and what is your vision for the future? This will keep you going. For this, you need presence of mind, and need to get rid of stress. You are the player, not the pawn. If you are a pawn, someone else is moving you, and you have no control. You have to be the player, empower yourself. And that's how the Art of Living programs can help you.

Question: What went wrong that so many people lack self-esteem and what can we do to lessen this effect?
Sri Sri: "Yes!+" and "Yes We Can" programs are good for that. We have "Yes We Can" programs in Europe. 140 youths from all over Europe participated. You should have seen how they were before the program and the change in them after it. They gained much self-esteem.

Question: How much freedom is to be given or restrictions to be put on teenagers?
Sri Sri: You have forgotten because you have crossed that stage. You do not remember the turmoil that you went through and which they are going through currently. There are so many hormonal changes taking place in their body. Shake hands with them and gently guide them through out of the turmoil. Teenage feverishness lasts only for few years. Not only physical but mental and emotional turbulence is

very high in them. After the age of three, children begin to experience the emotions like jealousy, possessiveness and these continue till teenage. Some people don't come out of their teenage turmoil at all. Mental turbulence is a big problem for them. Teenage is a tough time. It needs great patience to deal with teenage children. So, like a friend and philosopher, give them some space and at the same time put your foot down when required. You should not be too lenient all the time.

Sage *Narad* said, '*Yoga chitta vritti nirodha*' - '*Yoga* means silencing the tendencies of your mind.' '*Tada drustu swarupe avastanam*' - '*Yoga* is the skill of being established in the Seer from the scene' – to go within and be established in the seer. With this notion, there will be meditation. Then there will be *Samadhi*. Your mind will become totally calm and you will experience complete nothingness and emptiness for a moment.

Question: What advice do you have for parents handling teenagers?
Sri Sri: The 'Art of Living' Foundation has wonderful programs like 'Know Your Child' workshops which can help parents understand their children better.

Question: What is the role for the youth in this world?
Sri Sri: The world is currently facing some kind of stagnation. The youth have a great opportunity and can create a new world. A new paradigm shift is needed and it will start from India. Monetary prosperity is not actual prosperity. Inducing life, spirit of enthusiasm - this is what India gave to the world. Life is enthusiasm; life is love; life is compassion; life is creation and if these things die out in you then you will become a walking corpse.

Question: There are so many attractions and distractions but still youth are so bored.
Sri Sri:Youth are bored and it's their fortune. If they were satisfied,

then their growth would have stopped. When they are bored, then the quest comes in them. They are not satisfied with the things available. And this is the stage when they can take a step to look within - a leap in their inner journey; a step towards spirituality. An interest in higher growth gets kindled, when you are bored with things around. When you find the source of joy within, then obviously everything around is also reflecting the same source of joy and you are interested in everything. Continuous bombardment of stimuli on the senses can cause inertia. Inertia is a form of boredom. Again, when the *prana* level goes up, you move from inertia to enthusiasm.

Question: Dear Guruji, you talk about dispassion. Then what about passion?
Sri Sri: I think that people follow a career, business or profession just for money, and then money becomes their passion. Don't you think that the youth should follow their heart, passion and dreams? You should have a dream and a passion. You should follow it but not with feverishness. If you want to go to see a tourist place, you should go. You will make the necessary arrangements and visit the place. But if that gets into your head deeply and you keep on thinking about it all the time, then you will end up landing somewhere else.

Your mind loses clarity with feverishness. And you don't get right ideas or thoughts. Having passion and dispassion are complementary. Dispassion brings you centeredness, settles you down, and makes you calm. When you have a passion, it drives you to things that you want to have. Deep rest and dynamic activity are complementary. You cannot be dynamically active if you have not given deep rest to your mind and body. Someone who has never slept cannot feel energetic at all. In the same way, if you are not dispassionate, you cannot be passionate. You will only be feverish with desires and cravings in your mind and have no ability to act.

Question: Guruji, could you talk about the youth and what they can do for the society and the country.

Sri Sri: Youth implies enthusiasm, fun, a ready-to-do anything attitude, urge to create something new, etc. These are the qualities of youth. And all of you have these qualities.

It is important for our society that this youthfulness finds place in millions of hearts. We have to multiply rapidly on this front. Even if there are ten enthusiastic youth in a village, they can bring a lot of change there. They can remove any corruption and fanaticism prevailing nowadays. I will give you two examples.

There was a woman in Mumbai who knew the French. She came to me and said that she knew French and requested me to send her somewhere for doing service. I told her that she could go wherever she wanted and that we would make the arrangements for her. She went to the Ivory Coast. There was a conflict going on between Muslim and Christian groups there. There was a lot of tension in the villages.

This woman organized an 'Art of Living' course for all the people in one village. Then she organized a course in another village where people from the opposing group lived. She got both the groups together. The Christians went to the Muslim village and built a school there. The Muslims built toilets for the Christian homes. In this way, they became useful to each other and the whole conflict was resolved. All the problems were resolved in ten to fifteen villages. In 2008, the government of Ivory Coast rewarded the 'Art of Living' for the outstanding work done there.

Many of you would have heard of Kathewadi village in the Nanded district in Maharashtra. There is no signboard for any castes. There is just one board which reads, *'Divya Samaj Nirman'* (Divine Society). A few people took up the responsibility and organized *Nav Chetna*

Shivirs and meditation camps for six hundred families in this village. Earlier, it was a notorious village, but now there is *satsang* every day. There are no drug addicts or alcoholics in the village anymore. There are no liquor shops. Every home has a smokeless *chullah* (stove). The whole village is doing organic farming. There is a shop where there is no shopkeeper. The costs are printed on commodities. People pick up what they need and put the money in a box.

It was such a notorious village, and now it has become a model village. The Government has given them the honour of a 'Clean and model village' and also given them a monetary reward. A few enthusiastic youths changed the face of Dharavi slum, too. It is the largest slum in Asia. A quality school was started there. Children, who would wander on the streets, study there and pass with first class marks.

Delhi youths will also share their experiences of '*Meri Dilli Meri Yamuna*' programme. Even the government is surprised with their enthusiastic work. There is still a lot to be done by them. Each and every youth has this enormous power. Our youth have enthusiasm and awareness. There are many who are angry and enthusiastic. It is very easy to be so. But we want our youth to be enthusiastic and be aware at the same time – the youth who joyfully accomplish their goals. The goal is uplifting the society. Nobody should be suffering from starvation or depression. Nobody should be denied justice.

Question: The youth is so aggressive. We give them everything they ask for, yet there is no satisfaction. They are so hyperactive. How to mellow down such hyperactive kids especially when they are hurting others?
Sri Sri: Just bring them to the YES and YES+ courses. When the kids in Delhi did the course, their parents were wondering what we had done to them. They had become so nice. The parents had never thought that the kids would be so transformed after the course. The

same kids who had earlier said that they hated their parents started caring for them. They would send notes expressing their love and ask what they could do for them. There was a total transformation in the kids.

There are YES+ clubs in forty-three universities in the United states of America. In the Cornell University and several others, it is credit now. So, if you do the YES+ course and do meditation and the practices, you get credit. We will have to teach the kids meditation and ways to manage their own negative emotions. The world is recognizing this now and it will be good if India does, too.

Question: Who is your inspiration?
Sri Sri: There are two books you can read to find an answer to this. One is 'Guru of Joy' and the other is 'Walking the Path'. I would say my inspiration is every child. I want to see everyone to be like a child. Of course, I must say my mother was a great force. She was always concerned that I had to do better. Regarding anything that I did, she would say that I had to do better. So, she was pushing me all the time.

Question: There is so much competition in society that kids have no time to relax. There is a fear that they will not fit into society. How do we handle this situation? What is the *mantra* for excellence?
Sri Sri: I think you shouldn't push them too much. You should teach them to relax. That is why I said music, meditation and some games will help.

Question: Children don't care about their parents when they grow up. So many old age homes are there. Where do we fail as parents and what is your advice to parents so that this situation could be controlled?
Sri Sri: That is why I saying three types of trust are very important – Trust in oneself, in goodness of others and in the Divine. A little bit

of religious, moral and spiritual values, and the way you treat your parents and ask them to treat their grandparents can make an impact on them. So, you tell your children to take care of their grandparents. They will start doing that way.

Question: Today, children are getting more attracted to the western culture. My son gets annoyed if jeans are washed even after one wear. We have to pay an extra amount to get torn jeans. That is how he loves to wear them. How can we bring a change in this attitude?

Sri Sri: You know, all these fashions keep changing. So, don't worry. None of the fashion can stay forever. You create such awareness in your children and their friends. You inspire them to adopt some different styles. That is why I say that every parent has to be a good uncle and aunt. You can't care for your children only. You have to care for their friends. You should have at least six parties for your children at home in a year where you should interact with friends of your children. Call them all over to your house, have a pajama party, sit with them, talk to them, share stories, find out from them. If you spend one Saturday evening in two months this way, you can make a great difference.

Question: Please give guidance on parenting special children. What can be done for them through the 'Art of living'?

Sri Sri: You simply serve them. Don't pity them. The souls of people with special needs are in a different state. They are not in a sorry state. They have come to this planet just to take service. With this attitude, you should do service. Never sympathize – 'Oh poor child'. Children with special needs have come just to take service from you.

Question: How do we know children are into drugs or just moody?

Sri Sri: You can find this out. That's why it is important for you to know them and their friend circle. You will get to know what they do and where they go. You can keep a tab on them, especially teenagers. It is a very difficult time. They are undergoing such a biological change. So, they are not just satisfied with the love of their parents. Their body is discovering new things. They are looking for some love from outside – an emotional support, a physical pleasure. Their mind is in such confusion. So, to deal with teenage children is a big task. That's why we have the 'YES' and 'YES+' course, which is for teens. I tell you, these courses have opened up children in such a way which I cannot even describe.

In one of the courses in New Delhi, one thousand youths participated. We asked a them a question - "Whom do you dislike?" Eighty percent said that they hated their professor the most and seventy five percent said that the second most hated were their parents. In this country we say, 'Maatra devo bhava, pitra devo bhava, aacharya devo bhava, atithi devo bhava' - mother, father, teachers and guests are considered such ideals and manifestations of Divine. It is appalling to see the children start to hate them. We don't want violence and stress in our education system at any cost. We do not want the gun culture here as is happening in America. There is so much violence in class rooms there. Present year report says that campus violence have tripled in America from what it was in the nineties. So, it is very dangerous and we do not want this thing in India. That is why we need to bring moral and spiritual values, ethical values of compassion, friendliness and love.

Question: Guruji, my parents don't want me to be a vegetarian. How do I convince them?
Sri Sri: You should simply say, "I am going to be a vegetarian," finished, they will accept it.

Question: Guruji, I don't believe in God, is that bad?
Sri Sri: No never mind, at least you believe in yourself. You should know who you are. You believe in truth, honesty, love, compassion;

these are the qualities of God.

Question: Guruji, my parents love me so much that their love at times becomes suffocating for me. What do I do?
Sri Sri: It is a problem either way. Sometime you feel they don't love you, which is not true. Sometimes you feel they love you too much and it is suffocating. What to do? You know when you feel suffocated? When you want to do something wrong. When your consciousness says, this is wrong, I should not do it. That is when you feel the suffocation of your parents. It's good to be suffocated with that sort of attention. It's good to feel the guilt to do something wrong. You know it is a safety warning for you.

Question: Guruji, music is my life but most of the people around me do drugs and have bad habits. How can I keep playing and not being affected by all this?
Sri Sri: Stand your ground, it's good.

Question: Why is it always said not to watch action and horror movies? Do they have an impact on my mind?
Sri Sri: What do you think? Do you get nightmares watching horror movies? Then it is better you don't watch them. Okay you can watch one maybe in a year. Because the impact of it stays for a long time, it is better to avoid.

Question: Guruji, at times my parents hit me without a reason. How can I respect and accept them at that time?
Sri Sri: They can't do that without any reason. Tell them to do 'The Art of Living' course sometime when they are in a good mood. Coax them to come in a basic course and we will train them not to hit you.

Question: Guruji, when I took the course all the other kids shared that they had amazing experience but I did not experience

anything. I am very curious about it and I also want to experience it. What do I do?

Sri Sri: The fact that you are participating, you are already being benefitted otherwise you would not even ask this question. Yes, don't compare yourself with other's experiences. That person says he saw light and another person says I feel like this; then you start doubting your own experiences and questioning yourself. You should never do that, okay.

Question: How to bring up children in a competitive world?

Sri Sri: The world has always been competitive. In the past, competition was present on a smaller scale. It is much bigger now. We need to instill values. Even in the *satyuga*, there were *rakshasas* (demons). So, don't blame time. You do your part. Instill values in children.

Question: I want to commit my life to serving society. But my parents are insecure about this. How can I make them understand?

Sri Sri: Good! Explain to them, convince them. But if you're in the middle of education, complete it before you come here. Don't leave it halfway.

Question: How can we resolve the problem of increasing rates of crime and poverty?

Sri Sri: A shift from secularism to spiritualism is the solution to crime. This spiritual education must be given to children. Removing greed from the heart is the solution to poverty.

Everyone must take responsibility and think 'What can I do?'

Question: Dear Guruji, my son is now two years old, he feels insecure with other people. Do kids at that age feel that? How do I handle this?

Sri Sri: It may not be insecurity in the child. A two year old child would not be so insecure, it may be your own projection. Sometimes you project yourself too much on what the child is feeling or saying. Especially grand parents have a lot of projection on children. Grandpa will say, "My six month old baby looked at me and said, 'Grandpa you don't go for walk today, you stay with me,' and all that he was saying with his eyes." The baby doesn't even speak but grandpa feels that he says everything. A lot of it will be your own projection.

If you feel your child is a little jealous, sibling jealousy will be there. If you feel that, then you pat them and give them a little more attention.

Question: Sometimes, I am not happy with the school that my child is attending. Should I remove him from school and let him be at home?
Sri Sri: No, just because the school environment is not good enough, to remain at home is no good. Then children will become dull. We have to improve the systems in schools and this work is happening. That is why we are opening so many schools; we have opened around a 100 schools here in India.

Question: What is the best way to handle religious conflicts?
Sri Sri: Every child should know a little about all cultures and religions in the world. They will start feeling a connection with all the cultures. Every child should know a little bit about all religions like Buddhism, Christianity, Islam, Hinduism. They will grow up with a broad mindset.

I feel at home wherever I go in the world. I feel connected, and everyone can do that because we all have that need to be connected. In fact you don't have to make an effort, we are connected anyway.

I still remember an incident some 25 years ago, in Manchester, UK. A small girl came to me and asked, "Why cannot human beings connect with everyone else in the world?" I told her this is because we are so stuck in our identities. It's good to have identity but we have to grow beyond that.

Question: Why do parents expect so much from their children?
Sri Sri: You will come to know this in some years! But then you should remember that you also asked this question at some time in your life.

Question: What is your advice for parents as they get older?
Sri Sri: Parents should also become more happy and vibrant. Happier as you grow older! The older you are, the bigger should be your smile – satisfied and fulfilled that you have led a good life. Now, you only have to bless people of the coming generations. That is maturity. That is satisfaction. It comes when you become detached from day-to-day things. Wash your hands off anything that makes you unhappy. Take on your responsibility. Act for it but don't worry about it. People who act don't worry and those who worry don't act. This shift has to come. Otherwise, you keep complaining - so and so doesn't listen, daughter-in-law doesn't listen.

You should not go to your grave with complaints. Do only what you can. Stretch yourself little by little. We need to re-orient ourselves like this. Either we are complacent or we complain. Either is no good. Then you remain without doing any action. On the other hand, till the last breath, if you find fault with others, that is also not good.

The more we violate the laws of nature, the more the body experiences pain. These things should not bother you. If at all you have to be bothered, be bothered about the world.

Question: How can a multi-faceted personality be developed?

Sri Sri: Sometime back, our *Yuvacharyas* went to get license for a factory. They refused to pay any bribe. Without any anger and with full confidence they told the concerned person that they lived with the principles of the 'Art of Living' and that they would not give any bribe. That they could go to him fifty times if he wanted, but they we would not pay any bribe. That man gave them the license without any problems. I would want all of you to move ahead in teams like that.

You all have the time here to develop a multifaceted personality. You should gain as much talent as you can. We need to enhance our talents along with *yoga*, *pranayama* and meditation. Some people should frame talk shows - debating groups, journalism groups, etc. Those who are not good at public speaking should speak in public. Those who are bad singers should sing on the mike. Let those who don't know how to prepare food, cook. Then it may be a problem for them who know how to eat!

You just go on doing what you know. There is no joy in that. You should take it as a challenge to practice that which you are not familiar with.

How many of you felt energized as soon as you enter the campus (The Art of Living campus)? Many of you have travelled for long to come here. How many of you may feel that it is unusual that just entering a place makes you refreshed? Do you know why this happens?

(Audience: Because of you, Guruji!)

It is because people have been meditating here. Meditation keeps the energy high in the whole surroundings. This is the effect of meditation, knowledge and devotion. So, we need to keep this energy high, and to do that you should not miss the morning exercises.

We have different types of *yoga* - sports *yoga*, village women *yoga*, dance *yoga*, animal *yoga* and philosophical *yoga*. We can avoid any arguments, back biting or criticizing. If you feel any such thing in your mind, you can write it down and put it in the botheration basket. Suppose somebody in your room snores loudly while asleep! You definitely cannot stay for long with somebody who snores loudly. Either you use ear plugs or all the snorers are allotted one room. There will be an orchestra playing there! There is nothing wrong in snoring. Only one thing which needs to be ensured is that all the snorers go to bed at the same time. Then only can there be a symphony! (Laughter)

None of you are a guest here. All of you are hosts and you must act like hosts, and not guests. This is your place. You have to create a homely atmosphere. It is already there but you need to get that to yourself. So, everyone is a host, only I am guest here! Feel absolutely relaxed and at home. You anyway know that, no body needs to tell you that.

Those who want to write poems and articles should do all these things here. Rest everything is a surprise for you!

CONCLUSION

The youth have a great opportunity and can create a terrific new world. It is currently facing some kind of stagnation. A new paradigm shift is needed and it can emerge only from India. If a child needs both the parents' love and care, then it should be attended to first. Children's lives are very precious. The parents need to sacrifice some of their personal ambitions and comforts for their sake when they are growing up. Protecting and nurturing the family must be the first priority as far as possible. Teachers also have a big role to play here. Teachers have to set examples because the children watch them carefully. Their values are only partly learnt from their parents. The rest is learnt from their teachers. Children observe much more than adults. They observe everything parents and teachers do. They observe when you are calm and composed and when you are tense and unsmiling. They watch and imitate you.

We need to be broad-minded. Every child should know a little about the Upanishads, the Bible, the Quran, the Guru Granth Sahib and other holy books. Multi-religious upbringing, inter-faith education and inter-religious exposure will bring out much love and harmony. If all the countries spend even less than two percent of their budget towards globalizing wisdom, then every child in the world will grow up to be a happier individual.

The Art of Living

&

The International Association for Human Values

Transforming Lives

His Holiness Sri Sri Ravi Shankar

His Holiness Sri Sri Ravi Shankar is a universally revered spiritual and humanitarian leader. His vision of a violence-free, stress-free society through the reawakening of human values has inspired millions to broaden their spheres of responsibility and work towards the betterment of the world. Born in 1956 in southern India, Sri Sri was often found deep in meditation as a child. At the age of four, he astonished his teachers by reciting the Bhagavad Gita, an ancient Sanskrit scripture. He has always had the unique gift of presenting the deepest truths in the simplest of words.

Sri Sri established the Art of Living, an educational and humanitarian Non-Governmental Organisation that works in special consultative status with the Economic and Social Council (ECOSOC) of the United Nations in 1981. Present in over 151 countries, it formulates and implements lasting solutions to conflicts and issues faced by individuals, communities and nations. In 1997, he founded the International Association for Human Values (IAHV) to foster human values and lead sustainable development projects. Sri Sri has reached out to more than 300 million people worldwide through personal interactions, public events, teachings, Art of Living workshops and humanitarian initiatives. He has brought to the masses ancient practices which were traditionally kept exclusive, and has designed many self development techniques which can easily be integrated into daily life to calm the mind and instill confidence and enthusiasm. One of Sri Sri's most unique offerings to the world is the Sudarshan Kriya, a powerful breathing technique that facilitates physical, mental, emotional and social well-being.

Numerous honours have been bestowed upon Sri Sri, including the Order of the Pole Star (the highest state honour in Mongolia), the Peter the Great Award (Russian Federation), the Sant Shri Dnyaneshwara World Peace Prize (India) and the Global Humanitarian Award (USA). Sri Sri has addressed several international forums, including the United Nations Millennium World Peace Summit (2000), the World Economic Forum (2001, 2003) and several parliaments across the globe.

The Art of Living
In Service Around The World

(www.artofliving.org)

The largest volunteer-based network in the world, with a wide range of social, cultural and spiritual activities, the Art of Living has reached out to over 300 million people from all walks of life, since 1982. A non-profit, educational, humanitarian organization, it is committed to creating peace from the level of the individual upwards, and fostering human values within the global community. Currently, the Art of Living service projects and educational programmes are carried out in over 151 countries. The organisation works in special consultative status with the Economic and Social Council (ECOSOC) of the United Nations, participating in a variety of committees and activities related to health and conflict resolution.

The Art of Living
Stress Elimination Programmes

Holistic Development of Body, Mind & Spirit The Art of Living programmes are a combination of the best of ancient wisdom and modern science. They cater to every age group - children, youth, adults -and every section of society – rural communities, governments, corporate houses, etc. Emphasizing holistic living and personal self-development, the programmes facilitate the complete blossoming of an individual's full potential. The cornerstone of all our workshops is the Sudarshan Kriya, a unique, potent breathing practice.

- The Art of Living Course Part I
- The Art of Living Course Part II
- Sahaj Samadhi Meditation
- Divya Samaaj ka Nirmaan (DSN)
- The All Round Training in Excellence
(ART Excel)
- The Youth Empowerment Seminar (YES!)
(for 15-18 year olds)
- The Youth Empowerment Seminar Plus (YES+!)
(for 18+ year olds)
- The Prison Programme
- Achieving Personal Excellence Program (APEX)
www.apexprogram.org
- Sri Sri Yoga www.srisriyoga.in

International Centres

INDIA
21st KM, Kanakapura Road Udayapura
Bangalore – 560 082
Karnataka
Telephone : +91-80-28427060
Fax : +91-80-28432832
Email : info@vvmvp.org

CANADA
13 Infinity Road
St. Mathieu du Parc
Quebec G0x 1n0
Telephone : +819- 532-3328
Fax : +819-532-2033
Email : artdevivre@artofliving.org

GERMANY
Bad Antogast 1
D - 77728 Oppenau.
Telephone : +49 7804-910 923
Fax : +49 7804-910 924
Email : artofliving.germany@t-online.de

www.srisriravishankar.org
www.artofliving.org
www.iahv.org
www.5h.org